Ex Libris

Shirin Dastur Patel

◇◇◇◇◇◇◇◇◇◇◇◇◇◇

MR. DIMOCK
EXPLORES THE MYSTERIES
OF THE EAST

◇◇◇◇◇◇◇◇◇◇◇◇◇◇

Also by Edward Cameron Dimock

In Praise of Krishna: Songs from Bengali
(with Denise Levertov)

*The Place of the Hidden Moon: Erotic Mysticism
in the Vaisnaua-Sahajiya Cult in Bengal*

MR. DIMOCK EXPLORES *the* MYSTERIES *of the* EAST

EDWARD CAMERON DIMOCK

❖❖❖

ALGONQUIN BOOKS
OF CHAPEL HILL
1999

Published by
ALGONQUIN BOOKS OF CHAPEL HILL
Post Office Box 2225
Chapel Hill, North Carolina 27515-2225

a division of
Workman Publishing
708 Broadway
New York, New York 10003

Library of Congress Cataloging-in-Publication Data
Dimock, Edward C.
Mr. Dimock explores the mysteries of the East / by Edward
Cameron Dimock.
p.   cm.
ISBN 1-56512-153-8
1. India—Description and travel.   I. Title.
DS414.D56   1999
954—dc21   98-43901
CIP

10 9 8 7 6 5 4 3 2 1
First Edition

For Gerry Kelley, God rest him.
And for Mo Richardson,
Eric Solomon, and Andy Daland,
dear friends for sixty years.

Contents

◇◇◇

❖❖❖

PREFACE

It is hard, I know, in this day and age, to imagine having a car without a CD player, or a cassette deck, or even a radio, but I did. And after I retired from teaching at the University of Chicago in 1989, for several years I drove that car, a van, actually, back and forth between Chicago and Cape Cod six or eight times a year. Chicago was where my wife, Loraine, was still working. Cape Cod was where I had grown up, and where I was getting my father's house ready for us to move into when it was Loraine's turn to retire.

Although once in a while I had a human companion on those trips, such as my old friend A. K. Ramanujan, most often my company consisted of my German shepherd, Nikki. Among Nikki's many excellent qualities was, and still is, silence, and it is profoundly appreciated on most occasions. But there were times when Nikki and I tired, in our silence, of admiring the shapes of trees and the way the farmers worked their fields in various seasons, and our minds wandered. I don't know where Nikki's went, but mine usually went back to India, where I had lived with Loraine and first one and eventually five children, in the mid-fifties and early sixties, and where I had visited in various capacities two or three times a year ever since. And from those wanderings comes this book.

My memories were random, as memories usually are, so this book is, too. And my memory tends to seek out the pleasanter aspects of the past. While I have never ignored—indeed, it is not possible to ignore—the harshness and drudgery of some lives in India, and while scenes of violence and cruelty are burned into my brain, and while my academic life has been centered around the lofty structures and prismatic subtleties of some aspects of Hindu philosophy and religion, my memory would rather treasure the humor that is also very much a part of life in that country and culture. In Bengal, the part of the subcontinent that I know best, there is a long tradition of folktales, some of them very funny indeed, that twit the arrogance of kings and nawabs, the pompousness of the learned, the swagger and bluster of politicians, and indeed the very Bengaliness of Bengalis themselves. My memories are in keeping with that aspect of Indian life.

My pregnant wife and our two-year-old daughter and I first went to India in 1955, on a fellowship from the Rockefeller Foundation. I was to teach linguistics at the Deccan College in Pune (the name was then spelled Poona) and to study the Bengali language in Calcutta. Our little family (which, as the number of children increased to platoon strength, also took in an ayah named Rosie, a Bengali Christian) traveled back and forth between the two places by train. In something over two years we made eight trips across the country, spending two two-month sessions each year at the Deccan College and the rest at the University of Calcutta. Loraine was pregnant with our first son, and shortly after we arrived in Pune she gave birth to him, and to our second daughter a year later in Calcutta. We left India in 1958, and by the time we returned, in 1963, two more had joined the group. None among this mob of children remember anything about India except for the staccato chatter of the monkey-man's drum and the throat-closing sweetness of the tea cakes.

You will not find many Muslims peopling the book; there are several hundreds of millions of Hindus who are not here, either. What is here is an India that lives in a part of my mind, formed by particular senses and sensibilities, and idiosyncratic ways of looking at things. The India we'll wander through is not, in other words, the India that you might find today. For one thing, there are twice as many people there as there were in 1955, and I need not remind you of the implications of that. This is not to say that you cannot find the India of 1955 (or of 1755, for that matter) in today; you just have to know where to look.

❖❖❖

In which the author is shown by Manu
how to organize his life.

When the sages approached Manu, who was "seated with a collected mind," to ask him to explain the universe, he did so, and in great detail. Manu liked things neat, just as I do. We are what you call control freaks.

There are differences between us, too. Manu is a mythical figure (maybe several mythical figures), who compiled in great antiquity a compendium of law and custom that has directed the course of a substantial part of the civilization of the Indian subcontinent for several millennia. I am a real person, seventy years old, and have written a small book that remarks on parts of that civilization. Manu's name means "The Wise One," or even "Human Being." My name means "Crooked Nose."

Whenever I need advice on the correct thing to do, I turn to Manu's large book of laws. Manu, despite the fact that he was writing in India over two thousand years ago, is remarkably au courant, diverse and multicultural as he can be, and altogether up to the mark in dispensing advice about such varied matters as foods that can be eaten with impunity and ways of making restitution for violating your guru's marriage bed. Although perhaps less pithy than God's stony instruction on the subject of adultery, as transmitted to us through Charlton Heston, Manu's observations on this subject, as on others, are distinguished by a certain down-to-earth, expedient, human quality. At one point, for example, he suggests in his low-key way that "it should be known that there is nothing whatsoever here on earth more conducive to shortening life than doting on another man's wife." Unlike God, Manu is not authoritarian about it. You can tell that, being less than perfect himself, he has been subject to the occasional temptation. Indeed, his somewhat rueful tone hints that he may himself have been the topic of an aggrieved husband's comment, or perhaps worse.

Manu also tells me, to my dismay, that there are times when I should recite, and times when I should not recite. I should not recite when there is a fog or when arrows are whizzing by, or when I am on a horse, in a tree, on an elephant, donkey, boat, or camel, or when I am standing on salty ground. He need not worry, for the time being, at least, about arrows, or for that matter about the horses, donkeys, camels, or elephants, for as we shall see, my feelings about these and certain others among God's creatures are varied but strong. Trees, fog, salty ground, and boats, now, present considerably more difficulty, for I am writing while seated comfortably on Cape Cod, a place where it is virtually impossible to avoid any of them. And to top it off, here is Manu telling me that it is in any case not proper to recite until you have received the permission of your guests. To tell you the truth, I am not sure, in this situation, whether I am your guest or you are mine. I invite you, of course, to join me in meandering through various places and times in India, meeting entertaining people such as the ancient Indian sages Vishvamitra and Durvasa and the more modern sages Lenny Walsh and Suniti Kumar Chatterji.

I have been drawn toward India for as long as I can remember. I cannot say where the infatuation began. Perhaps it was a Shirley Temple movie or a Kipling story. I have always read what I could about India. But even so, when I first went to India in 1955, to teach and study, my books had not prepared me for what I found. I do not know that it is possible to be prepared, for India, and Hinduism in particular, offer a stupefying variety of forms. My battery of advisors, which included such experienced hands as Franchot Tone, Errol Flynn, and Basil Rathbone (without whose assistance Temple and McLaglan could never have retaken Kabul), had me primed for the tigers and ruby-eyed idols and cobras and

maharajas, of which more later. And my histories of philosophy had readied me for the lofty themes of the
Vedanta, that cool monism that so appealed to Emerson
and Thoreau and those hard-bitten transcendentalist
types as they chopped Walden Pond into cubes and
shipped it to "the sweltering inhabitants of Madras and
Bombay and Calcutta," as Thoreau describes the destina-
tion of his pond. (I myself don't understand why, if they
wanted ice in Calcutta all that much, they didn't just go
and slice up a Himalaya and slide it on down.) But there
are things not dreamt of in your philosophy: for example, as you are quietly sitting there having a cup of tea
with your friend Pratul Gupta in his book-lined Calcutta
study, chatting about unusual gods in Bengal, "Come
along," he is apt to say, "get your hat, and I'll show you
something different." You perhaps figure that Pratul, eminent historian and vice-chancellor of one of India's major
universities, would have something pretty good in mind.
And so you get into your jeep and head south about fifty
miles into the Sunderban. The name means "beautiful
forest," and indeed the Sunderban is more like it than
most other jungles, full of huge flowering trees with
lianas hanging down, and swamps, and Mowgli and
Rikki-tikki and Shere Khan and the others no doubt lurking back in there somewhere. And after a time, Pratul
might direct Ramkrishna, who is driving, to pull off the
track and stop beside a small terra-cotta temple. "This is

the home," Pratul might say, "of Daksin Ray, the Lord of the South. He is a tiger-god." And sure enough, inside the little temple there is apt to be a tiger, about three feet high, sculpted of clay, and beside it another image, a pale-faced figure in a red coat, white trousers, bandoliers, pith helmet, and an Enfield rife, standing at attention, as he has been doing for a century and a half. It may be an image of Kipling himself, for all I know. One hears people say that nothing is ever lost in India, that the culture just goes on, cheerfully adding to itself—just like the contents of my desk.

If it were not, then, for people like Manu to keep things in a semblance of order, India would, also like my desk, be an impenetrable jumble in which it is impossible to find your next doctor's appointment, to say nothing of the four expedient ways of accomplishing goals or the three ways to choose people for high positions in government. Manu has no such problems; he likes, as does baseball, to divide things up into sets of three or four and to store them neatly away where he can easily find them. He does this with stages of life, for instance. In the first stage of life, he says, you should be a student. As a student you are supposed to learn wisdom, that is, the way to grow older while damaging those in your immediate environment as little as possible (that is the way it used to be, at least; the core curriculum is now computer skills and multiculturalism). Manu suggests that you should take every advantage of this student stage, while your parents are paying the tuition: later on-the-job training is possible, but more arduous, for later on in life you will find yourself increasingly pressed for time. So even before Manu had told me to, I did all that for some years, with little success.

The second stage of life is that of the householder, and I did that, too, for a number of years. But then, says Manu, "When the householder sees that he is wrinkled and grey, and sees the children of his children, then he should take himself to the wilderness." "He can take his wife along," if she wants to go, but the bare minimum is that "he keep his hair matted and his beard uncut" (okay, that's easy), that he be "controlled, friendly, and mentally composed" (ah, well, so I lose one), and that he eat a lot of veggies (the Early Bird Special at my favorite local hostelry is roast beef with mashed potatoes, 2 veg, $5.95).

Having one day made the mistake of glancing into a passing mirror, and having seen that I am wrinkled and gray, taking to the wilderness is just what I have done, though Cape Cod is not the forest it used to be, what with the woodsy trails being clogged with cars bearing Florida plates and roots and berries getting harder and harder to come by. On the sandy hill where my grandmother and I used to pick a couple of quarts of blueberries in half an hour there is a development called "Blueberry Acres" and not a blueberry bush in sight.

The rest of it is second nature to me. The last time I had a haircut, the barber, nasty young snirp, said "Been cutting it yourself, haven't you?" I don't know whether he was aware that I also heard him mutter under his breath, "with a dull pair of hedge clippers, too."

So where I am is in *vanaprastha,* "living in the forest" or, as it is called in the West, "retirement," and so far it has been relatively painless. I am less confident about the next, and final, step, though, for that is *samnyasa,* or "renunciation." Manu tells me that any time now I can start walking in a northeasterly direction, "diligently engaged in eating nothing but water and air," until my body collapses. That does not sound attractive to me. Among other things, the course would put me several miles off the coast of Maine, on my way to Halifax, Nova Scotia, my grandmother's ancestral home, but a place I do not care to visit just now.

Manu doesn't seem to understand that to go downeast from here, as Cape Codders call it, you have to take a schooner. Walking puts you in the middle of the north Atlantic. But maybe that's his point.

PART I

❖❖❖

Passage

to

India

❖❖❖

Hey, Hey, We're the Monkeys

*In which the author is brought to speculate
on the nature of* Macacus rhesus.

In the fifties you usually traveled to India from Liverpool by ship, a ship that more often than not belonged to the Peninsular and Oriental Steam Navigation Company, an organization of British worthies that, raising an eyebrow at Rudyard Kipling, had as its motto *Quis nos separabit?* (And who's gonna keep us twains apart?) Their ships had for a good many years made it possible for tea planters, box-wallahs, civil servants, and others to ply their trades in various far-flung parts of the Eastern world.

These ships were sometimes named after Ionian islands such as Corfu, and leaning on the rails of them one would drink lime-and-lager and mentally prepare oneself for immersion in the new and frightening culture of the East by listening to the conversation of the old India hands:

"Now see here, Mandible, the best curry you can get is in the south. Shrivel your gizzard like a raisin."

"Stuff and nonsense, Ruffage. Good old Mughlai cooking is the thing. Make you sweat like a *kuli* and steam come right out of your ears. Keeps off the fever, too. Bearer! Two more pink gins for the sahib here and me, and a lime-and-lager for the Yank."

Our ship, *Corfu* would stop, for reasons of her own, at Aden, a flat, dust-colored town clumsily painted on a backdrop of similarly dust-colored mountains even then chockablock with hostile bearded folk with long guns. General Charles "Chinese" Gordon, the nineteenth-century general and cartographer who, like many of his kind, had been all over the map and was finally pinned down at Khartoum in the Sudan in 1885, had at one time decided that this was not the biblical Eden, and he was probably right about that. People must have gotten off *Corfu* at Aden anyway, for recently as I was moving Eugene Nida's *Morphology* from one place to another on my bookshelf, a yellowed mimeographed piece of paper fell out of it requesting "passengers finally disembarking at Aden kindly to attend the Surgery on Wednesday, 3rd August," probably for lobotomies. But sooner or later one reached Bombay, which popped up out of the ocean on a hot morning.

The continuation of our trip, to Calcutta, required the use of one of India's unique railroads and their equally unique railroad stations. Getting to the Bombay station from the ship was no problem, for we were shepherded there by an anxious group of Indians we had met on *Corfu*. Howrah Station, in Calcutta, however, was another matter.

Before we left for India, we listened tensely to our British friends and other experienced Western travelers, who all said, "Be careful to count your pieces of luggage in the railway station. Those *kulis* will run right off with it!" And sure enough, when we pulled into the Howrah Station on the train from Bombay, there were mobs of *kulis*, thin people who could otherwise be recognized by their faded pink shirts, dinner-plate-sized brass identification tags, and long pieces of cloth wrapped around their heads to keep them from getting flattened by the grand pianos they were sometimes requested to carry (I indeed knew of a Brit who, not trusting his grand piano to the railroad, hired a group of *kulis* to carry it from Bombay to Pune, a trip of 120 miles, much of it straight up).

When we reached Howrah, before the train had even come to a stop, a *kuli* lifted the basket with our small child in it and dashed off down the platform. My wife of course ran screaming after him, fighting through the crowds with the fury and valor that only a new mother under such circumstances can muster, struggling against the current to keep in sight the basket bobbing along on the waves of humanity, her pathetic cries being drowned out by the roar of normal station commerce. I was torn between a desire to help her out and one to remain where I was to make sure the rest of our belongings did not disappear. This did not, as it turned out, have to be a concern at all, for as I was negotiating with one *kuli* over the disposition of our worldly goods (except, of course, the basket with our infant son, which had already been taken care of), another would grab a bag or a box and dissolve into the crowd. Finally, bereft of senses, equilibrium—everything except one *kuli,* whose pink shirt I held onto tightly, the two suitcases in his hands, and one suitcase in my hand that was not clutching his shirt—I let the crowd, which was by this time surging the other way, carry me to the end of the platform, where I found not only my wife and baby but a reinforced battalion of *kulis,* waiting impatiently to get on with their day.

If you have recently arrived in India and come out of the railway station for the first time, the impression you get, which lasts a lifetime, is that every single soul in the country is on the move. If you stood there in front of the station, or anywhere else in the country, for five minutes, twenty-five hundred people of all sizes, shapes, and genders would pass you, no two of them dressed anywhere near alike, and they would be walking or riding bicycles, trams, rickshaws, buses, horses (sometimes with bridegrooms on the backs of them, preceded by ten-piece bands in tattered maroon and gold uniforms with no shoes, playing tunes that all sound very much like "Deep in the Heart of Texas" but that are in fact "Jingle Bells"), taxis, trucks with signs painted on the sides of them requesting everyone to PLEASE BLOW HORN, which drivers of other vehicles, eager to cooperate in every way, cheerfully do, pushcarts, and private cars. Among all these are camels, elephants, cows, buffaloes, dogs, donkeys, motor scooters, everything except the smaller animals being laden with rolled rugs, bundles of washing, pails of liquid hanging from both ends of arching bamboo poles carried on shoulders, steel trunks, water bags of skin, briefcases, shoulder bags, Calcutta cookers, trunks of trees, bales of cotton, small children—anything, in short, that can be carried, and some things that cannot.

I regret to have to say that contemporary India, though still crowded and hyperactive, is also more sterile. In the first place, the airplane, which is by its nature a prophylactic mode of travel, has become favored over the railroad as a means of transportation; but even when three 747s and one Ilyushin loaded with huge aggressive Russians arrive in Delhi at the same time (3:30 A.M., when you are at your absolutely lowest ebb), the airport crowds are more orderly than anarchic, the *kulis* fewer in number and forbidden to fight over your baggage (but now, perhaps as compensation, armed with heavy steel baggage carts adjusted precisely to shin level).

In any case, we finally did get to Calcutta, where, as I had lived a pure and saintly life, karma directed me to Lenny Walsh. Lenny Walsh was looking to rent out one of his rooms and advertised to that effect in the daily newspaper. He lived in a huge flat in an old colonial mansion that had been subdivided, its paved and now somewhat malodorous courtyard opening onto Chowringhee Lane. This lane is a thin and gnarled street that runs just to the east of and parallel to the monumental Chowringhee Road, ending dramatically against the New Market, or, more formally, the Hogg Market, a labyrinthine and magical place in which, I can say without exaggeration, anything in the world could, and probably still can, be gotten. Lenny's flat itself was on the first or second floor, depending on your system of counting, up a staircase fifteen feet wide but dark as the tomb, and consisted of five immense rooms stuffed with red plush Victorian furniture and intricately carved Burmese teak tables black with shellac and age, and hung with precisely the kind of heavy velvet drapes that mosquitoes love to congregate upon. None of the rooms except the two bedrooms was ever used except as passageways to the veranda, which was where the life of the household meandered toward its conclusion. Lenny himself was a thin, stooped fellow who looked at, or toward, the world with his head thrust forward and cocked to one side like an angry parakeet. He could hardly see, and his perpetual squint was so tight that in ten months of living with him I never once saw his eyeballs. The thrust of his head, which seemed so aggressive, really served to put him six inches closer to whatever was out there.

Lenny had lived a full and varied life, and he was not one to be either bitter or melancholy about his affliction. He had seen enough, he said, to last him several lifetimes, and he didn't care about seeing any more. As a sergeant with the Second Bengal Rifles in the fabled and oft-disputed Land Between the Rivers, or "the Messpot," as he called it, during World War I, he had been purged of fear by the unique experience of being left for dead of dysentery on a pile of corpses near Baghdad. He was lifted up by the hand of God, "who works in mysterious ways," said Lenny. "He saved me so that I could become a Crustean."

"A what, Lenny?"

"A Crustean! A follower of Crust, ye haithen! Blighted Americans," he muttered. "Haithens, the lot of them. Terry *bara peg* whisky soda *jaldi lao* goddamnit!" This last in full voice, for what he lacked in his visual faculty was more than compensated for by his vocal one.

Terry, I should explain at once for those who do not understand Lenny's Hindi, was the *nom de service* of a small grinning person from Orissa whose mother and fa-

ther had named him Muhammad Shah but who now occupied, as Terry, a significant place in Lenny's world,
which looked just like Calcutta but was in fact Belfast.
Belfast was Lenny's ancestral place, though he himself,
and his parents, and his parents' parents had lived in
India all their lives. His was a many-layered world, which
accounted for the fact that not only his English, but also
his Hindi and Bengali, had rich Irish accents. It was peopled not only by Terry but by Lenny's wife, Pansy, a pink,
smiling, motherly woman so pleased with the world that
it often seemed that she would explode with the sheer
joy of it; Johnny Walker Red in seemingly inexhaustible
demand and supply; tiny dust-mop-type dogs that yelped
incessantly as they chased bandicoots around the dark
stairwell; the few customers whose radios Lenny would
fix, largely by feel, to supplement his army pension; a
troop of monkeys; and now, my wife, small daughter,
newborn son, and me.

The monkeys, thirty or forty strong when the ranks
were full and enlistments closed, did not, for the most
part, live in the house, against the back side of which was
the Geological Survey of India. The survey consisted,
and probably still consists, physically, of a set of large and
very handsome British colonial buildings in pale yellow
stucco and green trim, beautifully maintained in spacious grounds full of royal and coconut palms, jacaranda
and jasmine, well-watered lawns and gardens of callas,

fronting on Chowringhee Road and, in the back, against our building, a godown and garage. This garage was merely an elongated lean-to that sheltered the numbers of World War II Jeeps and Land-rovers constantly under repair. On it was a corrugated tin roof, and on this roof were the monkeys.

It is next to impossible at any time to sleep much past dawn in Calcutta, for shortly after first light the bicycle bells begin to tinkle and the rickshaw pullers' bells begin to clunk and the trams' bells to jangle, and the crows and green Burmese parrots begin to discuss among themselves, over their morning rice and orange peels, the meaning of existence, and the taxi horns begin to belch and blat and the hawkers to hawk and the conch shells begin to moan in the Hindu houses, and the muezzin in the distant mosque to call the faithful to prayer. And in addition to all that, on our first morning in the city I was excited. But as early as I got up, I found that Terry had already been on the veranda for some time, rolling half-inch-diameter pellets from a basin of mud he had just brought up from the river. This was a matter of some bewilderment to me, but Terry merely grinned and indicated that Walsh-sahib would tell me about it in due course.

I left the house to keep an appointment, and by the time I got back to Chowringhee Lane the sun was high, and one hundred or more mud pellets were lined up on

the veranda railing to dry. Lenny, sitting on the side of
the veranda that opened to the back of the house, was
testing the stretch in the elastic of a formidable slingshot.
"It's you, is it?" he said, squinting in my general direction
and with two fingers fishing a Gold Flake cigarette out of
a round tin of fifty. He had just stuck this cigarette in the
corner of his mouth and lit it when, with a sound like an
ungreased armored division, forty monkeys came charging out of the palm trees from left to right across the
metal roof of the godown. As the first of the monkeys hit
the roof, Lenny loaded up his slingshot and, aiming by
sound, fired, and soon he was emulating Liprandi's Russian artillery at the Battle of Balaklava: as fast as he could
load he fired mercilessly into the flank of the charging
monkeys. Now and again one of them, stung, would stop
in his tracks and look aggrievedly around in the air, to see
where the missile had come from; others, out of sheer
high spirits, or to taunt Lenny, or happy because he had
missed them, turned somersaults and played leapfrog
with an exuberance wonderful to behold. And all the
time Lenny was shooting he was hollering "Take that, ye
little bahstuds! Get in Pansy's perfume, will ye?" It was
all over in ten seconds. The monkeys went whooping
away into some other part of the garden. Lenny as much
as blew the smoke from the muzzle of his weapon, laid it
aside, and requested his breakfast: "*Chota hajri lao* Terry
goddamnit!" All of this, I came to learn, constituted the

high point in Lenny's daily rounds, and quite possibly that of the monkeys, too.

Lenny's accusation did not stem entirely from the heat of battle, for at times the monkeys, true to their stereotype, would climb in the windows (screens were so rare in Calcutta then as to be almost nonexistent, and closing the shutters in the heat was largely unthinkable, so everything was open all the time) and get into whatever mischief happened to be there waiting for them. In his *cri de coeur* Lenny was referring to an incident of the recent past in which he had pushed aside the light curtain in the bedroom doorway to make out the shape of a monkey sitting at Pansy's dressing table dabbing face powder all over itself and fumbling among spilled bottles of scent.

My wife and I were new to all this and considered monkeys small sociable persons with grand senses of humor who lived, for their own welfare, in cages. It was therefore with considerable dismay that, shortly after one morning's skirmish, my wife, out of a window overlooking the tin roof, witnessed an epic battle over the leadership of the troop. The young male who won, after jumping up and down a few times and scratching himself in celebration, went galloping off, followed by the docile group that now seemed his to command. The old male sat there on the roof looking disconsolate, his shoulders hunched and his hands resting palms upward near his feet. My wife, who has little tolerance for the peculiar behavior prompted by the male hormone but great sympathy for old age and defeat, was so moved by this that she called out to the monkey in soothing tones and offered him a banana that was near to hand. The old monkey sat there and looked at her with ineffable sadness, obviously too upset to eat.

Later that day, as was the custom, I was joining Len and Pansy for a pink gin on the veranda before lunch. I had barely sat down in the Morris chair and was leaning back when all action was frozen by a scream from the bedroom. Since I was forty years younger than he and could see, Lenny beat me to the doorway by only half a step. There in the corner was my wife, her arms around our son, who seemed bemused by the whole thing; and there on the windowsill was the old monkey, giving little jumps and preparing to spike the banana he had in his hand, grinning maliciously and scratching himself in the armpits. When he saw reinforcements appear in the doorway, he spent a moment sizing us up, decided we were too much for him in numbers if not in intellect, and slid back down the drainpipe by which he had come.

Watching monkeys cavort mockingly around the fringes of humanness makes one understand how creative the divine hero Rama was in enlisting them in his epic struggle against the antigods, and how perfect is the scene in the *Ramayana* in which the monkey general, his tail on fire, bounds unpredictably through the great city of the enemy. The maneuver was also tried by the Chinese in the First Opium War: they attached explosive devices to monkeys and set them loose aboard British warships. The success of this is not known to me.

Hindus have long considered monkeys, like Rama's ally Hanuman, to be the epitome of courage, resourcefulness, loyalty, and strength, altogether indispensable to the gods in their constant struggle against arrogance. We in the West, on the other hand, seem never to have thought that highly of our simian cousins, considering them buffoons at best and dangerous, stupid pests at worst, and wholly inappropriate members of the family tree. I hold no brief one way or the other and remain content with Manu's observation that if you steal fruit, you become a monkey in a future birth. There is poetic justice in that.

On Curmudgeonry

❖❖❖

*In which the author ponders the qualities of
sages and the intelligence of animals.*

Some people would (and did) call Lenny a
curmudgeon, and while his dinner table
was not the "intellectual slaughterhouse"
that Groucho Marx once found at the Roundtable at the
Algonquin, there was a sufficiency of insult and usually
sham ill will, expressed in Lenny's three or four ungram-
matical but fluent languages, to qualify him. (Some people call me a curmudgeon, too, but what do they know,
those peasant swains and whoreson malt-horse drudges,
bawling, blasphemous, uncharitable dogs?)

A curmudgeon, according to the Oxford people, is
a churl or a carl, "a man correlative to a wife," "a boor
and the lowest form of freeman." A correlative of mine
sometimes uses these expressions, though in her scrupu-
lous fairness the reference is to "freepersons." When I referred the matter to M. Roget, the words "shrewish" and

"testy" occurred to him. While it seems to me that the former of these is feminine and the latter masculine, the Oxford people claim that in fact "testy" has nothing to do with masculinity, but that it is related to the French word for "head" and means, therefore, "impulsive." "What rot," says the correlative of whom I was speaking. "Testy is testy. Anything else is a male chauvinist opinion typical of a royal-loving, tradition-oriented bunch of shopkeepers." So it is clear to me that curmudgeonliness is not gender-specific.

Curmudgeons are not geographically limited in their range, either. The titleholder, in fact, is from South Asia, none other than a sage called Vishvamitra, "Everybody's Friend," who had extraordinary powers because of his asceticism. One of Vishvamitra's more memorable acts was to condemn the perfectly nice king Harischandra to an eternity of revolting rebirths, of which one of the more acceptable was as a worm in shit, because that king, preoccupied with the well-being of his people and the prosperity of his kingdom, neglected to wish him a good morning.

Vishvamitra was a hermit, for what might seem to be obvious reasons. Some of them are not so obvious, though. Vishvamitra had once been a king himself, and one day when he was hunting in one of his forests he saw, in the hermitage of a colleague named Vashistha, a very beautiful girl. As was the custom, he demanded that she be given to him right away. Vashistha, however, did not want to do that (the girl was not, to my knowledge, consulted), so they had a fight. Vishvamitra lost and retired, pissed off, from the world, emerging from his hermitage only every few minutes to rail at and vilify some startled passerby.

If you don't choose to believe that story, there is a variant one that says that while hunting, Vishvamitra stopped at Vashistha's hermitage with his whole army in tow (in those days, before they had automatic weapons, kings had to find other ways of eliminating the element of chance from the hunt). Vashistha, a hospitable sort, fed the whole bunch of them a magnificent feast, prepared within moments of their unexpected arrival. Impressed, Vishvamitra asked Vashistha how he did that. Vashistha modestly replied that he himself deserved no credit, that it was all due to Kamadhenu, the Wishing Cow, who happened to be in his possession. Vishvamitra, knowing a good thing when he saw it, made an immediate offer of a hundred million cows of the more usual variety, but Vashistha, taking the advice of his agent, turned him down. Thereupon Vishvamitra, like any good CEO on the verge of a hostile takeover, stated calmly that since he was king, everything belonged to him anyway, and he was taking this cow, like it or lump it. But as he was starting to lead the cow away, Kamadhenu stood right up on her hind legs, her eyes flashing fire (I have never, myself, seen a cow do this, but as we shall see again, Indian cows are often something else), and right on the spot gave birth to a whole army of fierce warriors, who proceeded to put the situation back into some kind of order.

And it was because of *that* that Vishvamitra became a hermit. Now and again he and Vashistha would meet in the forest as they were gathering roots and berries, or whatever it is that hermits do. Once, when their paths crossed, the words "sneaky, scheming, crafty, and treacherous" sprang into the mind of Vashistha, who was fond of reading his thesaurus, and he observed further that Vishvamitra reminded him very much of a heron, standing there in the water on one leg trying to deceive the fish into thinking that he was a reed. "Okay," said Vishvamitra, "if I'm a heron, then you're a kingfisher." And since they were sages, and their words the truth, the two of them flew away to a nearby lake, where they built nests and pecked away at each other until they were both covered with bleeding wounds, and everyone was sad.

Vishvamitra was also the father and guru of an inoffensive lad named Galava. Delighted at the academic progress his pupil-son was making, Vishvamitra decided that as a special favor he would demand no *gurudakshina* (the fee that students pay for their tuition, often in cows). But Galava, despite his genetic inheritance, was a generous and fair-minded fellow, and insisted that he pay something. So they bickered back and forth for a while, until finally Vishvamitra said, "Oh, for Pete's sake, okay, give me eight hundred horses, and make sure that every last one of them has one black ear." So Galava wandered around for a bit, trying to remember how he had left himself open for that one, until he came to the house of a king, who said, "I have a daughter named Madhavi, and she is so beautiful that anybody in his right mind would give eight hundred horses for her, so why don't you just take her along and make some trades?" So Galava did. But the first king that he and Madhavi came across had only two hundred horses of the required kind (they don't grow on trees, you know). Galava was depressed, but Madhavi tried to cheer him up by telling him, with either amazing considerateness or complete irrelevance, that she had been granted a boon whereby she would remain a virgin even after bearing sons.

Try as they might, the best they could do was six hundred horses, and they were both starting to get a little down when Garuda, a huge bird with a fowl mind, advised Galava to trade the six hundred he had on hand, plus Madhavi and perhaps a player to be named later, to his dad, Vishvamitra, in return for being let off the hook. Vishvamitra may have been cantankerous, but he was not stupid, and he took the deal.

So that is all about Vishamitra. We have not heard the last of horses, though, for recently I read a piece in the paper headlined "Police Horse Hit; Attacker Fined," which was about a man in Cincinnati who socked a horse for slobbering on him outside a tavern, something I had previously thought happened only in Mel Brooks movies. The man was not only fined but condemned to community service, from which there is no escape, for it is against the law in Ohio to assault a police horse or a police dog.

I am not sure about police horses, but it is pretty stupid to assault a police dog, for, apart from the legal consequences, these animals are usually large and have big teeth and, according to the latest polls, are rated just below border collies in intelligence. Your average German shepherd can take you apart and give you a lecture on anatomy while doing it. If you absolutely must attack a dog, you should probably choose an Afghan wolfhound, whose IQ, according to these same rankings, is not up there with the MacArthur grantees. It may be hairier, taller, and more distinguished-looking than you are, and outweigh you by fifty pounds, but you can probably outwit it.

Anyway, if anything is clear, it is that curmudgeonry is not affected by either time or space. I don't know that Vishvamitra ever went so far as to whack a peacefully slobbering horse, but I don't know that he didn't, either.

Rational Chaos

*In which the author is brought by Professor Chatterji
to examine the nature of cannibalism.*

India has been called a land of mystery. It is a
land in which middle-aged, highly respec-
table ladies will lead their ten-year-old children around the ancient temple at Konarak, which is
squirming with statuary of people coupling sexually with
other people and with a wide variety of nonpeople, in
attitudes that would blow your hat off. They are pointing
out to these children, I guess, the subtleties and intrica-
cies of the design. These are the same ladies who serve
you lunch with one end of their saris pulled over the
lower halves of their faces in modesty and hover in the
background until it is time to pile more food on your
plate.

India is confusing to some Westerners because things
there that seem to have a familiar or at least a recognizable shape disappear in the blink of an eye and form

themselves again as something slightly, or even dramatically, different. This can be disconcerting to one whose upbringing has urged him toward control of his environment and recognition of the substantial nature of reality.

Of the few places I have been, India seems to me to bring out best the basic order that lies beneath the world's seemingly chaotic surface, though, as chaos theory suggests, this is not always discernible by means of the raw senses.

There used to be, near the fire station on Free School Street in Calcutta, a place that can be described only as a dive, populated in the evening by "shippies," as they are called, and stunningly beautiful Burmese and Nepalese women. The dive was named Isaiah's, and, together with other monuments, it has disappeared into the omnivorous maw of the past. It comes to mind in this context because, like most other civilized establishments, it had a door marked MEN and another marked WOMEN. What was unusual is that both these doors led into a single large and tastefully white-tiled common room, appointed with a variety of porcelain furniture.

Recently my friend David Grene and I arrived in India about three in the morning, the time when most overseas flights arrive. As he surveyed the crowds—not mobs, I would remind you—of a density seemingly sufficient to make a big bang nearly inevitable, gathered patiently—not in line, exactly, but not pushing and screaming, either, the way they used to, in the railway station—around the immigration booths, he remarked "What chaos!" He didn't know then what chaos is. He repeated the remark, with annotations and somewhat more justification, at a later time, as our automobile tore through Calcutta streets crowded with all the Howrah Station items. It was also pitch dark, as nobody in Calcutta, for reasons I have yet to discern, drives with his lights on. (Wasn't it Dorothy Parker who said that the automobile has divided the human race into two unequal parts, the quick and the dead?)

But if there is chaos in Calcutta, it is a rational chaos, as we have seen in the case of Isaiah's unified accomodations, and it is also an educated chaos. For instance, take the poet and essayist Sudhin Datta, a man learned in many languages and at home with a variety of customs. He spent a fair amount of time in Europe, both in England and on the continent, and he had accumulated a very large and select library, in several languages, many of the books being first or autographed editions and valuable, about to be valuable, or at least of unusual interest. After a trip to Europe, Sudhin returned to his flat on Russell Street in Calcutta to find that it had been burgled. His collection of artifacts and other valuables had been left untouched, but the burglar had gone carefully through his bookshelves and removed all the first and autographed editions, together with whatever other books were to his literary taste. Sudhin, unflappable as usual, heaved a deep sigh and the next morning went to College Street, near the University, where many booksellers display their wares on the pavement. He bought his books back again, some of them with their inscription pages torn out, but at a discount, for of course the booksellers were aware of his reputation and approved of his work. Most cities in India seem to have a thieves' market —*chor* bazaar, it is usually called—but literary ones are to my mind unknown outside Calcutta. Come to think of it, there was a law student, several years ago, at one of our great American universities, who was caught lowering rare books from their depository in the library tower to a confederate on the ground, who would sell them to an eminent dealer downtown. That is the way to make money from education.

Anyway, I was once driving with a compatriot and friend named Gordon through a wasteland in the western state of Maharashtra. Gordon had been in India only a few weeks and was still convinced that the intense rationality of classical Indian philosophy applied to modern Indian life. We were driving along minding our own business when all of a sudden a herdsman and his goats materialized from the desert and started across the road in front of us quite as if they had the right of way, which they probably did. There was literally no one about, only buttes with forts on the tops of them whence Shivaji and other warlike Maharashtrians of some centuries ago had forayed against the Mughal Empire (which has been replaced, in the eyes of some of them, by the Congress Party). Gordon, thinking that the herdsman would control his flock, slowed down but did not stop. The herdsman, thinking that Gordon would control his car and keep things in their proper order, allowed his goats to cross in front of the car, and one of them got hit. It bounced up again at once, bleating impatiently, and pranced off to rejoin its cohort, which was by now foraging indifferently some distance away. The countryside, however, was anything but indifferent.

You know how English textbooks will give you an example of metaphor? For instance a textbook might explain that the figure of speech "the countryside sprouted people" depends in part for its force upon the fact that countrysides don't do that. Well, that's baloney. This countryside sprouted people—angry, shouting ones who banged on the car with their staves, obviously expecting to be satisfied for the psychological damage done to their goat by nothing less than payment in kind. Gordon, shaken to the core, unable to move the car forward because of all the people in front of it, took my loudly proffered advice and thrust a handful of large-denomination bills through a crack in the window, and while the crowd left the road momentarily to admire the money, took off like a rocket.

Looking back on it, I must assume that these people materialized out of thin air, for there is no apparent way into or out of the forts on the buttes. If these forts were not so inaccessible, they would make nice hotels, for that is what one does these days with old forts and palaces that have not yet disappeared into the abyss of time. Some of the results are as spectacular as their beginnings. In Udaipur, in Rajasthan, there is an ex-palace hotel on an island in the middle of a pleasant lake, all arches and inlays of colored stones and stone filigree that manages to retain despite its airiness the attar of the past. There are also, of course, a few palaces that are still palaces, with long audience halls with hanging crystal and walls lined with mirrors and the portraits of fiercely mustachioed warrior ancestors, and Kashmir silk carpets on the floors, and across a broad terrance a sweeping view of the curve of the Ganga. But the crystal is a little dusty and the carpets frayed; the few ancient retainers are uniformed in tatters and their swords are rusty, and in the dusty courtyard is tethered a symbol of the vast forests and innumerable animals owned in the past, a single battered skinny spotted deer.

India's past is imperial in many ways. Not only do the Buddhist empire of Ashoka and the Hindu empires of the Senas and Vijayanagara and the Muslim empire of the Mughals lie brooding beneath the surface of modern India, occasionally thrusting sharp remnants up through the layers of time, but the British Empire still lies very near that surface. And although the irritation caused by its presence is largely gone, the redness and an occasional itch remain. New Delhi is an intriguing and, I think, tasteful mixture of all of the above with the sheer glass faces of skyscraper hotels and office buildings. Scattered about the city are imposing ruins of fifteenth-century ramparts, spotlighted at night, dramatic enough in their power to let you feel somehow the presence of kings so fastidious that one of them had his tent moved twice, after a battle, as its floor was being soaked by the rising tide of the blood of slaughtered prisoners; yet these same kings were civilized enough to enjoy paintings made with brushes of a camel's single hair, or a single camel's hair, and odes to roses. And next to these ruins are so-called bungalows. The name suggests the small single-storied low houses of Bengal, but some of these, built by British administrators in Delhi, have thirty or more rooms, with deep, cool verandas and low balustraded tidy lines appropriate to administrators, and wide lawns for croquet and tea served by barefooted (by choice) servants in turbans and scarlet jackets with gold-colored sashes around their waists. And among these are the government office buildings, the Secretariat Buildings and the Viceregal Lodge (no hand-hewn rafters here, and perhaps no heads of unfortunate animals, either) and Parliament House being the most imposing, designed by the British archi-

tects Lutyens and Baker and built of the red standstone
that makes them so unmistakably part of the soil of India;
but unlike the jagged abrupt hills of Rajasthan, whence it
came, they have beautifully proportioned domes.

When you go to make a hotel out of your old building, you have first to decide whether you are going to fix
it up minimally, to keep out the rain but keep in the
echoes, or tear down everything but the facade and start
over again. Since many contemporary box-wallahs seem
to feel comfortable only if their hotel in Cochin is just
like the one they stay in in Columbus, the prevailing tendency is to do the latter. But some hotels were built as
hotels, and so remain. The Grand Hotel on Chowringhee Road in Calcutta is such a place. Off a huge teak-
paneled lobby with marble counters in the Grand Hotel
there used to be a dining room the size of the concourse
of Grand Central Station, with brass numbers on all the
tables, slightly run-down but very clean, and with very
alert waiters all over, solid silver service and heavy
teapots with thick cozies and white linen napkins stiffly
starched and fanned out in water goblets or shaped like
birds. Off one end of the lobby was a large garden where
one could sit under the stars and listen to the Goanese
band play sad romantic mondos, those soft-eyed melo-
dies born of a fortunate marriage beween Portuguese
and Konkani love songs, with trumpets in thirds, trying
to keep the palmetto fronds out of one's drink, and

watching the rats play around on the second-floor ledge. The monumental lobby, which made you feel as though you were approaching the throne of God, has now been splintered into homier "areas"; the dining room, too, has been made neat and modern; the ceilings have all been lowered and the atrium glassed in and made into a herbarium, where you now cannot pour the remains of your drink into the exotic foliage.

And yet, in that odd way that India has of never quite losing anything, as the Mughal and Lodi ramparts in Delhi seem quite comfortable beside the glassy facades, the Grand Hotel is still the Grand Hotel. Its cheeks are waxen and a little more rouged than they used to be, and the scars of some of its operations show, but the sum total is recognizable. I was in the place a few years ago. Still there is the corridor through which you would go to Prince's, a bar except on Sunday mornings, when it would get all decked out to serve a justifiably famous brunch. It was, therefore, on Sunday mornings after church, peopled mostly by British locals of the elite commercial and governmental establishments, with a few Bengalis thrown in for good measure or, in at least one case I remember, out of mischief. I went there one Sunday with Professor Suniti Kumar Chatterji, at his insistence.

Sunitibabu, as he was known by all and sundry, was one of India's greatest scholars, a startling polyglot as well as a brilliant analytic and historical linguist and writer. He was an immensely dignified man, heavyset, straight-backed, aristocratic, dressed always in an immaculate, crisp, Bengali-style dhoti (an ankle-length garment, one end drawn up between the legs and tucked into the back at the waist, to form a pair of loose trousers—a very graceful garment except when worn with dress socks and wing tips, a sartorial atrocity of which Sunitibabu was never guilty) and a beautifully embroidered Kashmiri wool shawl thrown dashingly over his shoulder. He was pretty intimidating: he had a high, sloping forehead, and his eyes were penetrating but hard to see well, because they were behind thick glasses.

Sunitibabu was a very busy man, his fourteen-hour days timed to the minute. The Sunday we went to Prince's, he was taking a day off. As he loaded up his plate for a second substantial breakfast, including a better-than-average selection of nonvegetarian dishes, I twitted him a little over the well known fact that Bengali Brahmans, of whom he was a prominent one, would trade a couple rungs on the karmic ladder for a well-cooked *hilsa* fish. Bengali Brahmans, I should add, are the sophists of the modern world and will argue cogently that fish are vegetables, first of all, and that, second, one does not kill them; one takes them out of the water and unfortunately, they die.

The room, a spacious one, was murmuring gently

with the subdued small talk and soft but tight-voiced commands to small children of well-to-do postcolonial Brits at breakfast. Professor Chatterji responded to my teasing in his well trained orator's voice: "Yes, I eat whatever is before me. You know, in Herodotus 3.99, I believe, there is mention of people in eastern India— *padaei,* he calls them—who eat human flesh. And so do I when I am among cannibals" (which is what a Hindu guest of ours remarked once, when one of our numerous underskilled cooks served him a piece of rare beef). The only sounds to be heard in the room were those of knives and forks being put down on plates, and the poorly repressed chuckle of my companion as he hungrily finished his brunch.

Most of the obvious colonial trappings are gone, renovated beyond recognition or ground down beneath the anger of those who would see only the repression of the Raj. But British India is in some places preserved with more affection than it is in the hearts of the renovators of the Grand Hotel. Zareer Masani's book *Indian Tales of the Raj* has a section entitled, with charming, warm irony, "Abide with Me." The title refers both to Gandhi's favorite hymn and to the fact that British India stays on in ways poignant and sometimes not without sting.

The ceremony called Beating the Retreat is a medieval remnant, coming to the Indian army through the British, when armies would withdraw from the field of battle in an orderly way, at the end of the day, to rest and await the next battle's dawn. Each year, the day after Republic Day, January 26, the custom is renewed. It takes place at dusk, opening with a Missing Man formation of aircraft trailing India's colors in smoke. That part of the ceremony can be seen elsewhere. What cannot be seen elsewhere are the stately red sandstone domes of the Secretariat Buildings, outlined in thousands of tiny individual oil lights, with the silhouettes of the Camel Corps still as statues on the ramparts against the stunning colors of the January sunset. And then you hear military music, with the skirl of the pipes and the blare of brass getting louder until over the top of the rise on which the Secretariats are located, against the brilliant orange sky, comes the turban of the Sikh drum major, and then the rest of the six-foot-seven-inches of him, with the music of massed bands swelling behind. After complex formations and music, and after the national anthem has been played, a quiet comes, and from somewhere in the towers of the buildings, chimes begin to play "Abide with Me," joined gradually by the pipes and brasses until on the last line of the hymn maybe a thousand instruments are playing, filling the open spaces as a great organ fills a cathedral. Then a silence once again, and to a light march the bands withdraw up the hill in an orderly way and disappear toward the last of the sun, retreating to the west, leaving the field to the echoes of Gandhi's beloved hymn.

They Also Serve

*In which the author gets looped on hashish and
has a dream about Ramkrishna.*

Many Americans in India, it would seem, have problematic relationships with people whose occupation is domestic service. These relationships are forced on everybody. They are forced on the servants because being servants is what servants do; their parents did it, and their grandparents, and everybody had found it a satisfactory way to make a living. They are forced on Americans because otherwise these Americans would have to spend the better part of their days at the market trying to buy fish and other vegetables; those who travel voluntarily ten thousand miles to do this in a language they do not always understand are few in number but great in heart.

It is also, of course, especially by the standards of most students and young scholars, an unheard-of luxury to employ servants, and thus it constitutes a crisis of conscience as well as economics for these young people and for other types of wanderers who are embarrassed to be waited upon outside of restaurants, and sometimes inside them as well. Their most extreme discomfort comes from being pulled in a rickshaw by a fellow human being. I must agree that it is a feeling that gnaws at you someplace deep in your gut, even with the realization that if these men were not pulling rickshaws they might not be working at all. In any case, to be waited on hand and foot seems un-American. Some people give up and sink down into the cushions and are swallowed up and never seen again. But almost all the visiting Americans, drawn to what they see as illicit comfort and embarrassed by having to recognize a previously unknown side of their personalities, are very touchy and difficult to live with.

Servants, of course, are entirely aware of this, and they would be fools if they did not take advantage of it. They therefore do nothing to discourage the feeling on the part of their employers or potential employers that overpayment is a balm for an irritated conscience. They also build wherever possible upon the realism with which British colonial families in India, more used to servants than we, perhaps, typically faced the problem: they recognized with an unflinching gaze into the eyes of truth that the cooks control the market prices, and that it is the nature of cooks to do so.

All of this may sound a bit exotic to you, and if you

have just this moment arrived in the city of Calcutta, you will be wondering how to make contact with the appropriate people. You should not wonder, for it is as true now as it has ever been that if you will look out your door you will see fifty people all holding out their letters of recommendation, or chits. There is a mysterious underground system of communication that alerts everyone in the subcontinent to the tactical movement of all European and American families into, out of, and within, Calcutta, but I have not been able to pin it down more precisely than that.

Some of the chits being held out to you by the people at your door are so old that they cannot be unfolded without the paper breaking along the crease, and they are signed "Pusillanimous B. Sprong, Deputy Collector, Kichuinagar District, Ret'd.," or "Von Klaustenberg Bahnhoff, Trade Representative, Weimar Republic," or "Gilet de Sauvetage, Emissary of the Sun King," and they all say something like "This man is a passable cook and entirely trustworthy, but if you have gold fillings it would be wise to keep your mouth closed when you nap in the afternoon."

These chits are presented with wide-eyed innocence, leaving it up to you to decide whether Gopinath, who is carrying the chit, really considers this a recommendation, or whether he is challenging you to a protracted duel of wits, which he knows you, secure in your cocoon of educational and cultural superiority, really think you can win. Sometimes you do win. We won one with a Nepali named Kancha, as gentle and kind a man as ever graced the earth, but lost one with Kancha's cousin, who came to cook for us when our regular cook fell ill. I forget this cousin's name, if indeed I ever knew it, for a little voice inside me (which gives me directions when I am driving and occasional moral instruction, and which I have, unfortunately only lately, learned to obey) told me to beware of this person; learning names establishes bonds, sometimes unbreakable bonds (my friend Gordon once made the mistake of naming a turkey— Dwight, I think—which he had bought and planned to eat at Thanksgiving; the turkey died, finally, of old age and obesity). This cousin seemed okay, except for a slightly demented cast to his left eye that was, however, not immediately noticeable, and it was not until his third meal with us that we realized that he could cook only two things: eggs and beef stew. Even that would have been tolerable for a while, but one day Kancha came to us, shaking his head sadly, and told us that we would have to sack his cousin, who had been found teaching our two-year-old son how to light "firecrackers."

The term "firecrackers" makes it all sound like innocent fun. But I am here, though barely, to tell you that in India they are more like real bombs. Like all other types of Indian fireworks, these crackers are homemade, at the

time of Kali Puja, in the autumn, when the fierce, aveng-
ing, loud side of the goddess is celebrated, and Calcutta
sounds like the South Side of Chicago on New Year's Eve.
Very few of the amateur munitions makers have a sense
of proportion about what they are doing. Powder is
crammed into clay containers that, when they explode,
scatter shrapnel over a wide area and leave big holes in
the street. Kali is the goddess of explosions and other
abrupt events, as I have suggested, and if you have ever
seen her image you will remember that her tongue is
hanging out to keep her eardrums from bursting. One
Kali Puja we were sitting peacefully on our veranda,
which extended out a few feet from the third floor of
the house, when a rocket came across, right to left,
missing the column, the railing, and our noses by inches.
It scared the hell out of us and left us in a state of quiv-
ering anxiety entirely appropriate to Kali Puja, besides
leaving us some glowing grains of powder to mark its
passage.

If you do not want to take your chances on the chit,
you can ask your friends for their recommendations.
Lenny recommended to us one of Terry's relatives, a
man impressively and also appropriately named Tipu
Sultan, after a warrior who had been a thorn in the side
of the British. After we had left India we realized that we
were missing a gorgeous prayer rug we had bought in
Port Said, went on to note that other things were missing

as well, and finally concluded that Tipu had robbed us blind in broad daylight.

While he was doing that, though, he traveled with us on the train back and forth between Calcutta and Pune quite a lot. In Pune he would cook a little, and, since the bungalow in which we lived was small and floored with a rough cement that needed little upkeep, he occupied himself by chasing rats with a bamboo staff. He thoroughly enjoyed doing this, and he had plenty of opportunity. The Deccan College, where I was teaching, is on a hill, and, thanks partially to the unsanitary food disposal habits of Narayanswami, who ran the canteen, was a place much favored by rats. While working late at night, one would often see them crossing furtively the band of light cast on the veranda through the open doorway. The problem, for so we considered it, would take on an added dimension during the rainy season, when the snake holes in the lower-lying ground by the river would fill with water and their occupants would come to the college for safety and for rat dinners. Our sweeper once found a six-foot cobra in our bathroom, which was connected to the main house by an outside—thank God—passage. It was some time before we got over our psychologically induced constipation, not to mention catatonia.

Between Tipu and the snakes, the rats had a lively time of it. They were difficult to discourage, however, and they continued to plague us in such numbers that more than once we woke at night to find one or several of them scrambling up the mosquito netting. This was a bit much, and so with some difficulty we got a couple of cats. Cats were at a premium in Pune, for what would seem to be obvious reasons, and maybe the cats we got were impaired in some way. The only stalking they did was of each other, and that in play; they never did seem to understand the nature of their profession. When they were not stalking each other, one of them would lie in the sun, occasionally opening one eye to gaze with mild interest at the end of her tail, which was peeping out from underneath a rear paw, twitching. Once in a while she would bat at it, and, even more rarely, would become furious at it and chase it around as though possessed. The other cat would lick its long hair and throw up. It got so that we almost preferred the snakes, which at least meant business, and, while neither companionable nor soft and fluffy, did their part in what had gotten to be an imperative symbiosis. One of them ate one of the cats, too, I guess, for she disappeared, and I'm sure she would never have left such a sinecure voluntarily.

IT USED TO BE proverbial that to live comfortably in Calcutta you needed eight servants. Most people today figure that is a few too many, but if you are going to have a car at all, a driver is necessary. Driving a car in India is not for someone of my jumpiness or generally frazzled nature (or perhaps yours either). When you are a student, a car is not a problem, for you simply never go anywhere you cannot get to by tram or bus. This is a mode of travel not only cheap and soothing to the nerves, but educational as well. If you happen to understand a little Bengali, for instance, you might well hear a conversation like this one on a Calcutta tram:

"Look at that [gustatorially peculiar white-skinned person]. You suppose he's a German?"

"Too skinny. He's probably a Brit. Americans don't ride trams."

Riding the tramway system in Calcutta is a unique experience in many ways. The trams, for instance, never stop for passengers or at any other time except to avoid plowing into the frequent crowds of people carrying red banners and blocking the tracks and chanting "__ __ __ __ *colbe na, colbe na,*" which means "[Fill in the blanks], it will not do." When there are no such crowds present, the trams slow down slightly at intersections to allow passengers to demonstrate their agility and preserve their slim figures by leaping on and off the moving platform. How women in saris do it, I don't know, but they have swimming races in saris, too, or so I understand. Once in a while one of these trams kills somebody (one killed Jibanananda Das, one of Bengal's greatest poets, a few years ago), but that doesn't seem to discourage anyone —the tram drivers least of all.

So if you need a car, you need a driver. We used to have one named Ramkrishna. Driving professionally in India is considered pretty macho, for the hazards are great, and the penalties for accidents even greater, so it should come as no surprise that Ramkrishna was also a wrestler and a weight lifter. All this would frequently put him on sides of issues different from those espoused by my wife. She couldn't stand his swagger, and he couldn't stand taking orders from a woman, or anyone else, for that matter. When stopped by the police for, say, going up a one-way street the wrong way (this was at a time when the municipal authorities were trying to bring some order out of the traffic chaos; after a while they pretty much gave up in despair), he would explain to the policeman that the sign had not been there half an hour ago. When he was instructed crudely to turn around and go back the other way, Ramkrishna would reply *"Agge ha,"* which means something like "I will do exactly as you instruct me, sir, and with your permission I shall do it instantly," and go along precisely as he had been going before, the policeman running ineffectually behind and blowing his whistle. My wife, however, could not believe that his indifference to authority was generalized but took it personally, and he ultimately left our employ and took up taxi driving, which suited him better anyway.

On a subsequent trip to India I happened to get into his taxi one night outside the Grand Hotel. While we were exchanging greetings, a policeman came along and told him in no uncertain terms that he was blocking traffic. *"Agge ha,"* he replied, and making a U-turn across three lanes of traffic under a sign that expressly forbade doing that, he took me on my way.

Another thing that did not endear Ramkrishna to my wife was that he decided, one Durga Puja, the great annual autumn festival of Bengal, to slip me a mickey consisting of considerably more than a normal dose of *siddhi*. *Siddhi,* a word used in a religious context for perfection, the final successful stage of spiritual endeavor, it is also a form of *bhang,* or hashish. At Durga Puja the drug is consumed in a kind of coconut milk shake. The slipping of mickeys has long been considered a first-class practical joke in India, though traditionally these mickeys have been in the form of the variety of thorn-apple called datura, which, says Burton in his *Anatomy of Melancholy,* "takes away all sense of grief and makes one incline toward laughter and mirth." So Ramkrishna thought that my performance under the influence of this hallucinogen would be good for a laugh, and maybe he was right.

On the evening of the last day of the *puja* lots of people get looped on *siddhi,* and it is available for an extremely nominal fee on your street corner. This evening is when the images of the goddess are taken to the river to be immersed, the clay of which they are made being returned to its source; it is the return of the goddess, who has spent the previous few days on her annual visit to her father's house (i.e., every home in Bengal), to that of her husband, the ascetic and often very weird god Shiva, in the Himalayas. Her departure brings great sorrow to all Bengalis, who are her family, and it is because of this unhappiness that people let loose.

That evening, then, my family, a couple of adventurous friends, and I spent an early hour or two wandering about north Calcutta, Ramkrishna driving and stopping now and then on street corners to make sure that I, especially, was never too parched. The *siddhi*-spiked drink tasted delicious, and, having absolutely no idea of its effect and being of a trusting, not to say naive, nature, I had quite a few. I felt nothing but good for a little while, but when we made our way through the crowds on the riverbank, the place was alive with goddesses. I mean it was alive: we were sitting beside some steps down which images were carried, to be immersed by swimming young men in the current, and these goddesses, some of them fourteen feet high, were swaying on the poles on the shoulders of the devotees and bending down toward me with their huge, staring eyes, and gongs were gonging and people were shouting and singing and the torchlight was glinting off the weapons in each goddess's many hands—and the next thing I remember is waking up, more or less, in my bed, with my experienced friend Jyoti leaning over me and saying to my wife, "Give him a lump of butter." What if anything the butter did I am sure I don't know. Something, though, brought me back from a place I did not want to be.

The other night I had a dream about Ramkrishna, whom I have not seen for fifteen years, but for whom I still feel affection (as well as slight intimidation). I have recently begun to keep on the table beside my bed a pen and a pad of paper on which to write down the profound truths that occur to me in the middle of the night. One night I woke up enough to write down something, and in the morning I saw that I had written, "Be sure to write down all the profound truths that occur to you during the night." That is what I call elusive. My wife has other names for it.

PART II

❖❖❖

The Wisdom
of
the East

❖❖❖

Shikar

In which the author is instructed
in the art of hunting.

Some time ago, a physician friend of mine named Herb Benson became interested in the fact that certain Tibetan lamas, as part of their discipline, are wont to spend their nights on freezing mountainsides with soaking-wet blankets wrapped around them as protection against the howling wind; these blankets are replaced by the lamas' considerate companions when they show signs of drying out. The lamas, it would seem, are able to raise their body temperatures, and Herb Benson, understandably, wondered how. He had also heard about certain of the other extraordinary powers that Tibetan lamas and certain Indian *siddhas,* or "perfected beings," have attained. These include, according variably to the texts on the matter that you read, being able to see buried treasure, being able to move anywhere undiscovered, the power, much sought-after also by medieval European alchemists, to transmute base metals into gold, and, of course, levitation. Other texts mention the ability to hear, constantly and without the radio on, sweet music or loud Vedic recitation; which of these transfixed my son as he stared into the open refrigerator, I never had the chance to ask.

Herb had lots of questions, and the primary ones pertained to levitation and the ability to move swiftly anywhere on earth. "Of course we can fly," said one of the old monks, "and tomorrow we shall demonstrate this for you."

The next day a group of young monks assembled. This surprised Herb a little, for in his experience the old monks are the adepts, as the discipline takes a long time to reach fruition. These young monks all sat in a row, and at the command of their guru they flexed their thigh muscles so powerfully that they all leapt, still in the lotus position, straight into the air. "That is a very impressive display," said Herb, "but what I meant by flying was traveling through the air from country to country."

"Oh," said the old monk, a twinkle in his eye. "For that we have Pan Am."

So DOING RESEARCH IN India is no pastime for the faint of heart, and patience is another virtue necessary for the successful hunter, or *shikari*. The manuscript, for one, is a shy, elusive creature, protected by its antisocial nature and other evolved mechanisms as well as by human conservationists. You must crouch quietly in your blind and wait. But I would urge you, when the opportunity comes, to pounce at once. Do not hesitate. And even then, you must be prepared for disappointment.

I once received word from a fellow traveler that a manuscript of a text that I was stalking had been located in a temple in a remote village of Bengal. This traveler had even taken a photograph of the colophon, the last few lines of the text, which often give the name of the book and those of the author and perhaps the copyist, and sometimes, in coded form, its date and place of origin.

The colophon of this manuscript showed it to be very ancient and rare, but word of it reached me at a particularly awkward time: I was scheduled to leave the country a day or two later. I was able to make arrangements with an able, experienced, and fluent friend, whom I shall call Rachel van Meter Baumer, as that is her name, and with the owners of some "portable" microfilming equipment (which in those days involved stands and reflectors and so on, all of it so heavy that a Jeep was required to transport it), to take pictures of the text. So, after I had bidden them Godspeed, they loaded up their Jeep and set off. As Rachel told me later, they traveled by the Jeep until they reached the end of the road, at which point they reloaded the equipment onto the back of an elephant, scrambled onto this elephant themselves, and swayed off into the jungle until they reached the bank of a broad river. There they put everything into a boat, crossed the river, and walked the few remaining miles to the village. The whole trip had taken a day and a half, but they had managed to find the right village with the right temple with the right manuscript. They were discussing with its guardian where best to place it for filming, when a small man dressed in a dhoti and a sacred thread came up to them and said, in English, "Madam and gentleman, what do you think you are doing? To do this thing you must first take permission of district officer. I am head-man of this village, and I have received no notice of your arrival from district officer." A lively multilingual discussion ensued, with references, in English, to the arrogance and general chutzpah of people with white skins, and in Bengali and Hindi to the type and number of occupants of the headman's marriage bed. But the headman remained unconvinced, and so my friends loaded their equipment onto their backs, the boat, the elephant, and the Jeep, and returned to Calcutta.

Rachel, well bred but stubborn, was not one to let the matter rest there. She wrote to the district officer, who after a couple of months replied cheerfully that, as it happened, he was going on a tour of the area that contained the village in question, and he would be happy to meet her there, together with the photographers, and smooth the way for her scholarly endeavor, of which he was much in favor. So they went through it all again, and as they were entering the temple for the second time, another small man stepped out of the jungle, raised his hand in a commanding gesture, and said, "Stop. I am Communist Party functionary for this area, and as you are looking like spies to me, I shall not allow you to proceed. You have been dropped, with your microfilm equipment, in black parachutes, in predawn vertical insertion, and are here in order to get the coordinates of my village, and to photograph, under guise of scholarship, our buffaloes. I shall not allow this."

The case made by my friends, even by the district officer, was of little effect, so they loaded up again and returned to Calcutta. Rachel's time in India was now also all but over, so she persuaded yet another friend, who, narrowing his eyes, agreed to lead a final charge. This time, care was taken that all political bases had not only been touched but jumped upon with both feet. Our friends were assured that no more obstacles would be placed in the speedway of knowledge, so the new team packed up and set off. When they reached the village, there, sure enough, were the village headman and the Communist official, all smiles and affability. They led the way into the temple, where the priest greeted them as if they were long-lost relatives and brought out the manuscript, in its cover of fine cloth (for it was a sacred object, deserving of care and respect), to have its picture taken. Such, in fact, was the veneration in which the manuscript was held that the top folios were unreadable, as it had for three centuries been smeared daily and reverently with vermilion by the hands of the devout. As a matter of fact, of the 360 folios that the manuscript contained, the top 359 were unreadable. The bottom one, with the colophon, was quite clear.

IT IS TRUE, TOO, according to Manu—and it is often pointed out in India—that the lives of ascetic scholars do not mix well with those of kings. The ascetic Caitanya would not go near any place where a king might be lurking in the bushes; on the other hand, ascetics do not pay tolls on ferries, thus putting a considerable strain on royal treasuries. I must say that certain kinds of ascetics do not stand in lines, either. I was, once, after a long wait at the Bombay airport, finally getting to the front of the line leading to the inspector of carry-on luggage, when two American Hare-Krishna types pushed their way into the line ahead of me. When several of us pointed out this discourtesy, one of them looked down his long nose and said, "We are monks." They were many other things, too, if you could believe the people in my immediate vicinity. In any case, when it came to my attention that another text I was tracking had hidden itself in the house of a certain maharaja, it gave me pause.

It happens that in eastern India, many of the royal families who once ruled states both large and small, independent of British India, claim in fact to be one extended royal family that traces its origin to Rajasthan. The subfamilies had, at independence, lost all their great wealth and power but none of their dignity and bearing. I had a friend who was a Rajkumar, a prince, in one of these families, and he was a prince in more ways than one. He was a man of great intellect and imagination, a metallurgist, tall and of military bearing, handsome with a small goatee and well-trimmed mustache that made him look like a benign Mephistopheles, and with a calm and steady gaze that was both daunting and appealing: you were drawn to this man but understood immediately that he did not suffer fools.

He made an exception in my case, and as he was affable and sympathetic to my cause, it took little persuasion to get him to drop a note to his cousin, the Maharaja of Konosthan, whose library contained the manuscript I sought, requesting that I be given permission to examine it. So I set off at once, and I had soon ensconced myself in a small hotel near the palace and sent a note to the maharaja announcing my arrival in his city. I received a note in return, telling me to show up at the palace the next evening at six.

Twitching with anticipation, I did as directed. I was shown into an antechamber and given a cup of tea and the leisure to examine the daguerreotypes of prostrate animals scattered about the walls. These animals mostly had boots firmly planted on them, these boots being filled with the feet of the maharajical ancestors, and the heads of the largest of the animals were sticking out of the walls. There were also faded portraits of musta-chioed military persons with jewels in their turbans star-ing sternly at me. I was not terribly disturbed when the servant who had brought the tea returned, eventually, with the news that the maharaja was slightly indisposed, and that I was requested to reorganize myself and appear at the same hour the following evening.

I was somewhat disturbed, however, when the scene repeated itself five times. Both my patience and my wal-let were growing thin, for while the hotel was cheap, it was not free. After a certain amount of pleading to this effect, I was finally shown into the royal presence, seated in one of those curly, uncomfortable Victorian chairs, and required to make conversation with a rather morbid man who was drunk out of his mind and obviously had been so for a week. But I managed to make myself un-derstood, and after trying futilely a few times to snap his fingers, he got it across to the servant that we wanted to see the manuscript I had described. It was stored in a long cylindrical tube made of pressed paper. The manu-script itself had once been made of palm leaves but was now, as we found when the servant unscrewed the cover on one end of the tube, a pile of dust about the consistency of flour.

The Sanskritist Hans van Buitenen used to say that 90 percent of Indian literature has been eaten by white ants. These ants may be a nuisance, but no one can deny that they have digested a prodigious amount of learning.

You Are What You Eat

❖❖❖

*In which the author is compelled to come
face-to-face with curry.*

As the vegetarian movement in the United States grows in numbers and vociferocity, people should be aware that there is much to be learned from a parallel and classically attested movement that has taken place over the centuries in India. For indeed, despite the conventional understanding, vegetarianism has not simply always been there in India but has come to its place of prominence over time. Let me introduce the subject with an instructive story.

One day in Calcutta, as I was eating my usual breakfast of two single-fried (i.e., sunny-side up) eggs—this was before the days of cholesterol, and besides, our cook could not cook anything else—our friend Pradeep Sen wandered in. Most of the time Pradeep, like some other members of the landed gentry, drifted like a cloud around

South Calcutta, following his nose and the winds of fancy, but a visit to us so early in the morning was rare. At any rate, he sat down at the table with me and said, "You can't eat those eggs!" Always on the qui vive, I examined them with considerable care, but I could find nothing wrong except that they were as stiff as if they had been cooked in laundry starch, as perhaps they had. But I had eaten them that way many times before and come away relatively unscathed. I inquired as to the reason for his remark. "Because," Pradeep replied, "they will make you hot-tempered and passionate." And indeed they did.

You never know when you are going to be blindsided by a cultural concept and left twitching on the artificial turf. I removed my keen, piercing stare from the eggs and placed it upon Pradeep, who was by this stimulated to further speech:

"Animal food is hot food, you know. It creates *pitta* in your system. *Pitta* is what you call bile. Bile helps in your digestion and also creates heat, sight, imagination, and courage, you know, but when it is in excess, it is like anything else in excess, you see: bad. Food with fiery quality is increasing this *pitta*. Therefore, no, no, I beg of you, do not eat those eggs."

Despite the fact that it was eight o'clock in the morning and therefore 102 degrees, I turned a cold shoulder to his entreaties and continued to slice my eggs into their rigid component parts. But, of course, he was right. Hindus always are in such matters.

There are usually two reasons given for the necessity of vegetarianism. The first one is more prevalent on this side of the water and reads, roughly, that you will turn into what you eat. If you eat animal flesh you will turn into an animal. This principle is at work in certain ways of thinking about karma, and the logic is inescapable: there is no explanation other than a diet of asparagus for those people whom one occasionally sees walking loose about the streets with bright green hair. Also, the leather jackets suggest that the asparagus was not of the first, most tender, crop.

The lighter, sweeter, and less crude concept, which Pradeep Sen was giving shape to, is that it is all a matter of proportion. He was not (at least, I think he was not) suggesting, as my mother used to, that if I continued to eat eggs I would turn into an egg, or perhaps a chicken; he simply meant that animal protein would bring about an imbalance in my system (already a volcano of seething passions), causing it to replace digestion by indigestion, vision by blindness, coolness (a quality quite as highly valued by Hindus as by young Americans) by heat, courage by fear, and so on. But things are rarely so simple, and what would at first seem to be a straightforward binary opposition is in fact the reverse: ambiguity and complexity are increased, which is good, and the fact that even negatives have positive value is wryly acknowledged in the rhyme that suggests that the Englishman is ten feet tall and mighty because of his cannibalistic gustatory habits, which are also celebrated in the name of his excellent gin.

So all that is about the passionate kind of heat. There are other kinds of heat, too, and one of them is when you take a mouthful of curry and your sinuses suddenly feel as though they are being scoured with a Brillo pad permeated with sulphuric acid. Despite other derivations you might have come across earlier, the fact is that *curry* is a Tamil word used to connote the sauce that is poured over rice. What we think of in English as curry is actually the blending of spices known as *masala,* a name apparently derived from the Arabic for either "materials that are conducive to good" or "a torch," which seems to me far the more likely. One of the usual primary ingredients of Indian curry is chili. It is not often recognized that this hostile plant, and its name, were brought to India by the Portuguese—one more in a long series of atrocities committed by European hegemonists. India, however, has always been an absorbent culture, and it has taken in stride the onslaughts of the Huns and Mongol hordes, and the Dutch, French, and British merchants and military, as well as the Portuguese and ravening American students, and gone smilingly on its way—in this case merely observing good-naturedly that eating hot things in a hot climate brings the inside world into equilibrium with the outside one, cleansing the nose and eyes along the way.

Curry, which comes into English from Tamil via Portuguese, is in its consistency similar to what Sanskrit and Pali often render by the word *sup,* in translation, "soup." The whole matter brings to mind one of my most vivid memories of my first stay in India. When we were in Pune, my wife and I shared a bungalow at the Deccan College with our friends Bill and Elizabeth Bright. When we first went there, one of the things that impressed us mightily was that the bungalow, being all verandas and open rafters and windows, was full of birds, mostly sparrows, flying back and forth, making nests in the eaves, chirping happily, and in general trying to make us feel welcome in their home. My wife and I exclaimed in delighted tones about how nice it was going to be to share a house with birds. Bill Bright had been in India longer than we had. "Wait until they shit in your soup," he said, sourly.

In India it is not only what you eat but how you eat it that has an effect on the nature and structure of the cosmos, despite the fact that some analysts still think table manners and collateral considerations are "culturally conditioned." For example, if one were to follow the traditional instruction in the matter, one would not sit at table with anyone who was wearing indigo-colored clothes, as there is a possibility of pollution in that dye. Dinner with any of the queens Elizabeth, therefore, would be a gamble. In fact, to be strict about it, since you are never entirely sure who it is that you are sitting at table with, it is far safer to eat alone. Those around you may be guilty of all sorts of sins, which you will absorb with your food. It is also said that if you eat in public you quickly become bereft of wealth, and that is especially true if you feel compelled to pick up the check all the time (this is also a sign of insecurity). You are also not to eat food on a boat, or on the back of a camel, which is a good example of empiricism becoming dogma. Nor should you ever accept food from a spy or from an actor, for obvious reasons.

There are also many rules about how much you should eat. An ascetic should eat eight pieces of whatever it is, a hermit sixteen, a householder thirty-two, and a student an unlimited number.

To return for a moment to Bill Bright's remark, the texts of social regulation and conduct, such as Manu's, have, so far as I know, nothing to say on the subject of guano in your curry; it is, in fact, the one topic that they have somehow missed. They do go on about food that has been cooked with hair in it, or ants, or the limbs or tails of mice, and food that has been picked at by a crow (i.e., in modern Calcutta at least, all food that is not zealously guarded by a regiment of fierce Gurkhas), or smelled by a cow. If the food is completely polluted, of course, you have to throw it out. But if there is a remnant that is clean, it can be purified by sprinkling it with water that has been contained in gold, repeating a prayer over it, and giving it to a goat to look at. I don't know whether or not you have ever had the opportunity to gaze into a goat's eyes; they are empty and baleful and yellow and cruel, and they would scare whatever pollution remained after the water and the prayers right the hell out of there.

It is commonly understood that these days Hindus are vegetarians, though in the case of Bengali Brahmans, the definition of "vegetable" is sometimes a little loose. The texts had Bengali Brahmans in mind when they said that fish that have the heads of men or of elephants should not be eaten; Bengalis did not catch many of those anyway, and they still do not. But it is less well known that vegetarianism is a relatively late reform of the culture, the result of a puritan campaign such as the one being carried on in the United States today regarding smoking. The fact is that in ancient India the eating of meat was not only okay but prescribed in certain circumstances. In narrowly defined ones, it still is today. As I drilled deeper into the rock-hard remains of my eggs, Pradeep continued:

"It is alright, you know, to eat meat, but only when

the animal has been dedicated to the goddess, for then the animal goes right to heaven. When prayers are said before the animal is killed and the animal knows it is going to be killed in the name of the goddess, it becomes calm and none of its fear and anger remain. So none of the fear and anger gets into your system, but instead the calm and resignation that the animal feels gets in, and that is a good thing, isn't it?"

That is indeed a good thing, and the Hindu culture is one of kindliness and sympathy, though it may be possible to locate an individual here and there who does not live up to the ideal. Nor would it be cynical to observe that in India, as in all cultures, certain compromises are dictated by necessity. At one time, an offering of the meat of the rhinoceros, especially if it was made by a Brahman sitting on the hide of a rhinoceros, satisfied the spirits of the Fathers for all time. Offerings of animals other than rhinoceroses, to say nothing of rice and butter, just don't seem to cut it as well.

The major reason, though, why India is vegetarian, has nothing to do with text or tradition, or moral conviction, or even the rational argument that the giving of milk and the ploughing of fields can keep you going for a long time, whereas you become hungry again soon after your steak dinner (one could wish that New England fishermen and others, who scrape clean the Banks, destroying thereby not only the fishes' future but their own, would understand this principle). The major reason is an understanding of the fact that only arrogance makes us think that we are at the top of the food chain. Indian texts say that we are not only eaters of food, but also food ourselves, for the gods and for death. This may be why they say that you should not speak ill of food. By no means should you ever, for example, send a dish back to the kitchen, complaining that it is underdone.

Diu Ever Think of Me?

◇◇◇

*In which the author is shown a little island
and communes with the spirits.*

Out of deference to the principles of Mahatma Gandhi and perhaps also because you are what you eat and maybe what you drink, too, the State of Gujarat on the northwest coast of India, Gandhi's ancestral home, is dry. It is arid in both the geographical and the bibulatory senses of the word. There was in fact a time, maybe twenty years ago, when all of India was dry, and there are still times when certain states are, and people just over the border in other states make lots of money. At yet another time, having two dry days a week was tried as an experiment. On these dry days it was impossible to buy liquor except by going up to the shuttered door of the wine shop and asking for it; the proprietor, who would be standing outside that door awaiting the opportunity to be of assistance to his thirsty fellow countrymen and other passersby, would dart inside and emerge after a minute holding a bottle-shaped object disguised as a fat rolled-up *Times of India*. Glancing both ways, he would slip it to you for the market price plus five rupees.

These attempts to impose morality, of course, not only failed to do that but caused huge revenue losses, and they have by this time generally been stopped. As in some areas we in the West have not profited by India's experience, so in this they did not profit from the American one. It is as if the two cultures had been sitting in the same room, each of them carrying on a separate conversation with an invisible companion.

In any case, the Deccan College in Pune was in the state of Maharashtra, which was a dry state when my family and I arrived there in the fifties. Next to the bungalow in which we lived there was an empty field of perhaps three acres. In this field, one night when we were all asleep, there sprang up like a mushroom an encampment of gypsies. These gypsies looked just like their ancestors must have looked centuries ago, before they started wandering off toward Europe, and as they look in operas today: dark, strikingly handsome, fancifully dressed people in red bandannas and multicolored skirts, with big gold rings in their ears, and horse-drawn wagons painted in primary colors. They made their living selling trinkets and moonshine, and they had come to the right place, for as Americans relatively fresh from the boat and panting for exotica, we were anxious to throw our money at them in exchange for their trinkets. Also, I, at least, had not come to India prepared for enforced detoxification, so I thought I was in luck with the moonshine. Unfortunately, after the first sip I became convinced that detoxification was preferable to death, and I had, despite extreme pressure, little difficulty in withholding my custom from these enterprising, creative, attractive, but gustatorially challenged people. The stuff tasted like Liquid Plumber cut with lemon juice.

In Bengal, I might add for the sake of you ethnological comparativists, what they call "country liquor," famed in folk song and story, is made from the flowers of the beautiful *mohua* tree, gathered and distilled by lithe, bare-breasted Santal women, moving through the green shadows of the jungle like graceful ghosts. It tastes like battery acid. A gentleman by the name of Forsyth once wrote a book called *The Highlands of Central India,* in which *mohua* was described as "ardent spirits, resembling to some degree Irish whisky." He may have been thinking of some other highlands, and aye, there's many as would dispute him on that one, too, ardent or not.

Although some other parts of Bengal were from time to time afflicted with prohibition, the tiny formerly French enclave of Chandernagore struggled mightily to preserve its Gallic right to the exudations of the grape and whatever else has juice. Other notable exceptions to

the general rule were the formerly Portuguese posses-
sions on the west coast, namely Goa, Daman, and Diu,
which, even after they were taken over by independent
and arid India, were allowed to retain the ways forced
upon them by their former regents.

Hindus have long objected to the use of alcohol, and
their texts of moral and social regulation, the Dharma-
Shastras, state lots of reasons for that, many of them
valid. But in the usual Hindu combination of pragmatism
and puritanism, the texts also say that if you do happen
to take a drink, you can atone for it by eating only every
fourth meal and standing all day and sitting all night for
three years, after which, presumably, you would be too
tired to lift a glass for a while. Islam was much more
rigid about it, though some of the Mughal emperors,
among others, were known to hoist a few when the occasion warranted. They were, in this, not discouraged by
the vast numbers of Europeans who were for some reason roaming about the subcontinent in the sixteenth and
seventeenth centuries posing as technologists, usually ar-
tillerymen or surgeons or both. Surgery aside, one would
think that the firing of artillery, especially sixteenth-
century artillery, would be work for clear eye and steady
hand, but Niccolao Manucci, a Venetian adventurer and
jack-of-all-trades who spent some forty years at various
Mughal courts in the mid-seventeenth century, tells us of
an English artilleryman who consistently shot wide of his

mark, until somebody brought him a bottle. After drain-ing it, he shot the eye out of a gnat, so to speak, and there-after assured himself of a continuous supply of booze. What happened to his liver, Sgr. Manucci does not record.

So, Goa and these other Christianized places were, and are, as we speak, unending sources of moderately priced spirits and of a magical wine that puts in liter form most of the major philosophical questions; when you wake up, you do not remember much about your past lives, and you wonder who you are, exactly, and how you got to be where you are. Time and experience sometimes reveal the answers to those questions, and sometimes not. Goa is otherwise a very picturesque place, with Old Lusitania in its very marrow, and to the north and south of the city and seaport, and up the many inlets and rivers and backwaters that make that whole part of the coast so intriguing, are miles upon miles of beaches, yes, with coconut palms bending gracefully to-ward the water, deserted but for gaily painted sewn fish-ing boats pulled high on the sand, with fishermen sitting around them mending their nets. Indian developers, who are quite as greedy as their counterparts in other sections of the world, have of course taken note of this pristine and very beautiful area and are trying their level best to put luxury hotels on it all, with swimming pools right next to the beaches. There are some stretches of beach still unscathed, and these are filled with nude European and American hippie remnants, being looked at by middle-aged, middle-class Indian ladies and their ten-year-old children.

Goa also contains a large number of churches, some of them quaint and white stuccoed and likely to pop up in unexpected places, others curious though impressive local adaptations of the great buttressed gothic and Romanesque cathedrals of Europe, uncomfortably hunched like rigid, cowled friars among the swaying hips of the jungle palms and radiant color of the forest flowers. In one of these cathedral-type churches lie the remains of St. Francis Xavier, a small, wizened person 490 years young and, I am sorry to say, looking it. He is in a glass case, made necessary, I have been led to understand, because in the not-too-distant past a devotee, in a fit of passion, bit off one of his toes.

The little island of Diu, which is north of Goa, on the coast of Gujarat, cannot compete with any of this grandeur, as it has only a stone replica of either Vasco da Gama or Bartolomeo Dias. (I get them confused because they are both short, pugnacious persons with slightly crossed eyes.) The last time I saw him, whichever one he was, he was standing somewhat apart in a courtyard in which had been collected the shards of several buildings that had been deconstructed into these component parts by the ships of the Indian Navy in 1961, fourteen years after the rest of India had become independent from Britain. What the tiny Portuguese garrison could have been thinking during those fourteen years, as they stared out at the vast, well-trained, well-armed Indian army and navy, to say nothing of the air force and marines, can only be imagined. At some point, the Indian journals of the period suggest, the garrison began acting in a hostile manner. There may have been, of course, the usual combination of pigheadedness and confusion. Whatever happened, it was not helped by our then–Secretary of State John Foster Dulles, who was going about the world busily proclaiming that Goa and these other places were "provinces of Portugal" and generally indicating that like his later colleague Henry Kissinger he knew neither what century he was in nor what place. Dulles's mistake was not nearly as serious as Kissinger's, whose tilt to Pakistan in 1971 dumped the eight ball right into the corner pocket, to be followed rapidly by all eleven others and the cue ball. But it was serious enough, for people were killed, and there is an obelisk by the docks in Diu dedicated to the many and varied Indian regiments that took part in quelling the vast and rabid Lusitanian horde.

This tiny island is still reached by a big, lumbering old lateen-rigged dhow that plies back and forth over the strait. Just as with the buses in the cities, this ferry crowds on more passengers than is safe, or even reasonable, and people hang onto the bulwarks and braces on the outside of the ship, getting in the way of the sailors trying to work her, dodging the good-natured kicks of the helmsman as he tries to make room for his huge tree trunk of a tiller to swing. Somehow he rounds this twenty-ton dhow right up under the pier as if it were a Sunfish, and the passengers disembark, chattering loudly in an attempt to be heard above the crackling of the luffing sails.

The ferry docks on the southward side of a town around which you can walk in an hour. It is an hour spent in sixteenth-century Lisbon. The streets are parallel to the waterfront or at ninety degrees to it, straight up and down the hill that is the island, and lined with multistory houses of wood and stucco leaning toward one another as if in conspiracy, as they go upward. And on the waterfront, occasionally you will find a sidewalk café where you can sit, with dry Gujarat on several sides of you, and have a bottle of beer or a glass of rum, provided you are willing to share it with the flies, who have never teetotaled, and the timid cockroaches, who come out from under the table and feel thoughtfully around to pick up the vibes of the situation before joining the group. There will also probably be a bunch of soldiers who have come to relieve their boredom by trying to communicate with you in all available languages, and a group of children who have rarely felt the kind of excitement that is to be had watching you eat *pakoras* and drink Kingfisher Beer.

While you are eating your *pakoras* and chatting with the soldiers and children, you can look out at the single ancient dhow tugging gently at her anchor in the harbor. She may have come from Hormuz, as her ancestors had done, or Mombassa. And as early as the seventh century, there would have been ships from China swinging there beside her, taking a breather on their labored way to the Persian Gulf. You might also do as I did and buy a bottle of Old Monk XXX Rum against a rainy day, for although there may not be a cloud in the sky, it is best to be prepared.

To the west of the town, on a point, is the fort, or what remains of it, with walls and dungeons and chapels and cells for monks or prisoners or maybe both, built in 1535. Actually, several times before 1535 the Portuguese had requested permission to build a fort on the spot, and though they were turned down by the local ruler, they were given, to assuage their feelings, a rhinoceros. The rhinoceros was kept for a while in the king's zoo in Lisbon and then sent on to Pope Leo X. While it was on this journey, it drowned in a shipwreck, and only its carcass arrived in Rome. Leo X, it is reported, was ecstatic, and in 1514 issued the bull *Contra nasacornes.*

When, some time after, we were at the airport leaving Gujarat on our way back to Bombay, the guard searching my briefcase took out the half-empty bottle of rum, held it up to the light, sighed, and put it under his table. I of course objected, contending that I had purchased it legally and also that I was in the process of taking it out of the state, not bringing it in. Neither argument carried much weight, and I hope the inspector had the courtesy to toast my good health that evening.

What's in a Name?

◇◇◇

*In which the author gets ticked off and
finds his silver tongue.*

When you live for a time in a place like India (not that there is any other place like India), it is possible to forget certain things about your native culture and even language. After a couple of years in India, for example, I had forgotten that it is necessary in New England to identify male individuals by their middle names. Henry Wadsworth Longfellow, for instance, is called that to distinguish him from Henry Saltonstall Longfellow and from his cousin on his mother's side Henry Lowell Saltonstall Longfellow Wadsworth. The habit is perhaps English, for I have noticed that many Englishmen feel utterly naked without their middle names, as did Arthur Darby Nock, for many years a singular professor of the history of religion at Harvard. Professor Nock was a stout, rumpled-type Englishman with many pairs of small glasses that he would interchange unpredictably, an umbrella, mustard on his waistcoat, amazing erudition, and a bowler hat, or "Darby" (though it is possible that this last is wishful thinking on my part).

Arthur Darby Nock lived for a good many years in an oak-paneled suite of rooms, with a brick fireplace, in Eliot House. At least, my memory tells me that it was oak-paneled; all the rooms were lined with bookcases, and all these bookcases were filled with books, and every bit of counter, table, and floor space was also piled or lined with books, except for a few square feet in front of the fireplace, where there was a rug. The story, which I have no reason to question, goes like this:

One cold November day, Arthur Nock was lying on this rug, utterly starkers, a cheery fire upon the hearth, checking out what Irenaeus and them had to say about the Book of Acts, when the door opened and in walked the chambermaid (yes, it used to be that way at Harvard, and for all I know still is), feather duster in hand. "Jesus Henry Christ!" she observed. Arthur Darby Nock propped himself up on one elbow, pulled his current pair of little glasses down to the end of his nose, looked at her over them, and replied, "No, Madam, but His humble servant, Arthur Darby Nock."

It was Professor Nock who first pointed out to me that in some traditional Hindu ways of looking at things the relationship between words and the objects they represent is natural and eternal. Arthur Darby Nock was himself in name, nature, and substance Arthur Darby Nock, and no one else, and that's the God's truth.

The news about the relationship between word and referent came as a relief to me, for I had squandered a good deal of my youth wondering how Adam could have dreamed up names for all the many creatures of the world. I mean, when he was confronted by what we have come to know as a dog, how did he know whether to call it "dog" (or *chien, kukur, hund, svan, canis,* etc.) or, for that matter, "cat"? Even though he had a lot of names to choose from, very few of them, early on, being taken, if he had thought up a name a minute for sixteen hours a day, every day including Sundays, it would, according to the science writer Chet Raymo's calculations, have taken him about three hundred years to finish the job.

It is just not reasonable to ask anyone to put in that kind of time (there were not enough of him to unionize). But if a dog is a "dog," that is, if the creature and its title are naturally identical, the problem dissolves. All Adam had to do was look at the animal, open his mouth, and the name popped out. It was a no-brainer.

The Hindus have thought this out pretty thoroughly, as they have most things, and over the centuries have come up with a number of interesting sidelights and practical applications. They stress the importance of the notion that language has more than an arbitrary relationship to the natural order of things and the powers that make the world go round. To illustrate this, they tell the story of a sage who was in the process of uttering a curse that was intended to bring divine wrath down upon the head of his enemy (sages are like that). But in the recitation he tripped over one of the syllables, said the wrong thing, and by that mistake brought the whole shooting match down upon his own head. The moral of the story, of course, is "Get it right, and get it right the first time." My mother used to put it another way, namely, "Be careful what you say, it may come true; also stop crossing your eyes."

So, to avoid this kind of disaster, Hindus have become, over time, very meticulous about their pronunciation, and also about storing things accurately in their memories—sometimes long and complicated things like the Vedas (the ancient books of hymnody and ritual; the Rig-Veda, for instance, the oldest of the four sets, is made up of 1,017 often lengthy hymns). "Things have gone okay for the past several thousand years," one Hindu would say to another, "they could be a lot woise. So we have to do things just as we have always done them. Don't upset the apple cart." If you pay a visit to a traditional school in India, you will hear classes of children reciting various texts not only one end to the other, but backward, sideways, skipping every other syllable or line, or one line left to right and the next one right to left—in general proving that they have a pretty good grasp of whatever the text at hand might be. As for myself, the task of trying to commit to memory, undertaken at the strongly worded urging of my English teacher, Hamlet's brief but poignant musings on his excessively solid flesh and resultant desire to diet, was difficult to the point of impossibility, and these days I have more than enough trouble with my telephone number.

But sometimes things stick in your mind and stay there whether you know it or not. My family and I once arrived in Calcutta from Pune before the building containing the flat we had engaged was finished. We decided, therefore, to go away for a few days while the workmen put on the final touches, that is, the walls and roof. We decided to go to the Southeastern Railways Hotel in Puri, in the next-door state of Orissa. This hotel is not at all like it sounds it might be. The railway is indeed the proprietor, but the hotel is an old-style British colonial place where civil servants and others from Calcutta used to go to get away from the heat and the pressures of the city. It is all open verandas and talky crows that come swooping down to take the toast right off your plate at teatime, and spacious rooms so breezy that there is no need for fans, ever, and a library and a billiards room and all the other amenities of moderately gracious colonial living, and cheap to boot. It is right across a broad white beach from the Bay of Bengal, which was, at that time of year, just after the monsoon, all glorious surf and fishermen in tall cone-shaped hats woven of palm leaves and painted white, for they were serving as lifeguards and fighting one another for the privilege of "saving" ecstatic, giggling, nearly naked fat Russian ladies in the pounding surf (they much preferred this to going miles out onto the tumultuous bay in a little outrigger canoe). It was, in short, a thoroughly enjoyable way, for both us and the fishermen, to pass the time. But eventually we were forced to face the fact that we had to return to Calcutta.

Indian trains sometimes used to run a little late, and this was one of those times. By the time we got to Howrah Station, found a taxi, and made our way across to the southern end of the city, it was nearly midnight. And there, gleaming in the full moonlight, was our house: walls, roof, everything brand-new, marble floors glistening, paint fresh and smelling like milk. The only thing missing was the furniture, including beds, for which we had contracted before leaving for Puri. Our children, exhausted after the long train ride, had an understandable need for those beds, and they expressed it loudly and at length, as I did myself. In fact, I spent the next four or five hours expressing it, leaning over the veranda railing, building up a head of steam, and puffing on three or more cigarettes at a time. As the sun was peeping over the horizon, from down the street came a rattling noise. It grew louder and louder, until finally around the corner came a bamboo handcart, creaking and groaning on its wooden wheels, pushed and pulled by three piratical-looking men, on which was piled all our furniture. As two of the men began to unload the furniture and carry it up the two flights of stairs, I requested a word with the foreman. I took him aside, and when I opened my mouth, out poured a stream of Bengali invective the like of which I had never heard before and have not heard since. On and on it flowed, the air around us getting bluer and bluer, until every snatch of angry or obscene language I had ever heard, and which my subconscious had obviously stowed away somewhere to await just this opportunity, had come forward into the open and shaken its fist under the nose of the poor *kuli* before it. This *kuli* was standing with his palms flat against the wall behind him, staring at me with wide eyes. As I finally ran out of gas, he said to me in a voice soft with wonder, "Sahib, what beautiful Bengali you speak."

Once you start to memorize things, it is evidently difficult to stop. One time, I was sitting in the room of a friend of mine in Calcutta, drinking a quiet cup of tea and chatting about these very matters. The chair I was in was against a wall of books on all kinds of subjects in all kinds of languages. "Everything I read I automatically memorize," my friend said. "It is not a matter of being born with an abnormality such as a photographic memory, but of training a perfectly ordinary one." Sensitive to the scepticism radiating from my every pore ("Bullshit," was, I think, the way I expressed it), he went on: "Reach behind you, take a book at random, tell me its title and the number of the page you open it to." He began at the top of the page I identified, in the middle of a sentence, and recited the rest of the page without a pause. Consider: if we in the West had this kind of training, we wouldn't have the need for so much print, and we might have some forests left. Nah.

So the Hindus are aware of the power of language and of the usefulness of memory, and they have been able to transmit some of their books for thirty-five hundred years without ever writing down a word (some, indeed, consider the reading of written books to be an obstacle on the path to knowledge, a position with which some of my grandchildren agree). The next logical step is the consideration that control of language is control of power. We are talking spells and magical formulas here, and magic, as you know, can provide you with a wide range of perks, such as control of the three worlds (hell, earth, and heaven, or past, present, and future). Hindus, therefore, have been as concerned about it as anyone else. The best kind of magic words, everyone seems to agree, are those that are beyond cognition, those that are meaningless in the ordinary sense of the term. A Buddhist text on the subject says that if a meaningless word such as *phat* is repeated five times at three different periods of the day, even an ass becomes the master of three hundred works. *Phat phat phat phat phat.* This text does not say whether the ass gets to choose the three hundred works. Hindu texts offer, in return for your repetition of the meaningless formulas, to paralyze your enemies, bring you young ladies (I am sorry, but that is what the texts offer), or, as I mentioned, get you control of the three worlds.

Phat phat phat phat phat.

Sometimes, if what you are looking for is particularly difficult to obtain, the texts will recommend certain rituals to go along with and enhance the power of the formulas. One suggestion is that you go to a cemetery or a cremation ground at midnight to get the corpse of a non-caste person or a person who has been killed with a sword or bitten by a snake, wash it and worship it (the formulas are there in any number of ritual handbooks), and then duck, because if you don't the Power that you have summoned is going to hit you square on the honker. If for some reason you cannot manage all these activities, you should give a good dinner to a Brahman. I might add that also inherent in the formula *phat* is the power to become proficient in learning without any study; this is the obvious reason why it has become popular with the very young.

We in the West are not unfamiliar with all this. We have the early Christian belief that the names of Egyptian demons contain first-class power. If, as an early Christian, you happen to have a bit of this esoteric knowledge about you, you can, if you want to, fly. And though opinions seem to differ, from text to text, as to the number of repetitions of a meaningless formula necessary for maximum efficiency, most seem to feel that one hundred thousand reps a day is a nice round number, and also builds up your abs. It is not a coincidence that this is also the number fixed upon as the optimum number of repetitions by most advertisers on television. And this is only one of the many ways in which classical Indian thought has influenced our modern Western life.

Phat phat phat phat phat.

I don't think it works.

Give and Take

*In which the author learns about generosity
and also Edward G. Robinson.*

One of the sterner among the books on social behavior, the Dharma-Shastras, suggests that a rich man who does not give gifts appropriate to his ability to do so should be drowned with a millstone around his neck. While we all have our opinions about Bill Gates, most of us would agree that this is perhaps too harsh, as our minds boggle at the thought of gifts commensurate with his wealth. I recall reading that at a wedding celebration in Bombay (the family of the bride, a well-off group, hired the outdoor football stadium for the party) each of the several thousand guests was given a golf-ball-sized pearl set on a golden tee, all of them inserted into a green made of a vast emerald, or of something in any case that the less privileged among us would consider extravagant.

Anyway, generosity is a feature of the culture of India,

and it is looked upon favorably by those who set the rules. I learned this first when I was lecturing at the Deccan College. My wife had just given birth to our son at a local hospital (Lady Dorabji's Boyoboy Nursing Home, I believe), and the morning after the event I stood as usual before my lecture class of seventy or eighty students. Before I could begin to talk, one of the students in the front row raised his hand, rose, and said:

"Sir, I am speaking for class, and we would remind your good self of the custom here in our India that when a son is born, the father of that son distributes sweets to his friends, who in this case are also his students. Yes, yes."

And so, after class, and after quoting Manu to the effect that overeating, and going around with food on your hands or mouth, destroys merit, besides which, people hate it, I got on my bicycle and went to the sweet seller to discuss with him the matter of fifty pounds of pumpkin *halwa,* which he agreed would not set me back more than half my month's salary. He was happy, and the students were happy, too, until I reminded them that it was also customary to present the newborn with gifts, twelve days after the birth, and that I would accept the gifts in my son's name, and that gifts appropriate for a teacher were fields, gold, cows, horses, umbrellas, shoes, grain, clothing, or vegetables. They looked at me as though I were talking in Burushaski. They did give me a beautiful shawl, though, some time later, satisfying the clothing requirement.

It was the same look of bewilderment that I had noticed on the students' faces when they listened to a colleague of mine expound to them on the issue of juncture in the English language. As an example he was using a song popular at the time, the lyrics to which went "Mairzydoats andozydoats anlillamziedivy," and he would occasionally break into this song and skip about the lecture platform. It soon became clear to Gordon that nothing was registering, and he moved on forlornly to the vowel system of American English.

When I look back on it, it occurs to me that it may not have been the problems of juncture that the students found puzzling, but the fact that their ears were attuned to the sounds of British and not American English. They did of course quickly adjust to new accents, for languages are not a problem in a country where tri- and even quadrilingualism are not unusual. There is in fact a great curiosity about and concern with language. It is said that the Mughal emperor Akbar had two overriding ambitions in life: one was to find the source of the Ganges, and the other (which he shared with the Egyptian Pharoh Psamtik, if my memory serves me, and with the Linguistics Department at MIT) was to find the source of language. To solve the latter problem he locked twelve infants in a house for twelve years, with instructions to those who served them that never a word should be spoken around the children. It was a major question, and perhaps a source of financial speculation, whether the children would emerge speaking Chaldean or Hebrew or Sanskrit. Of course, they spoke none of the above. The *Akbarnama,* the history of Akbar's reign, says that in the chapter called "The Twenty-seventh Year" the children were "timid, frightened, and fearful, and such they continued to be for the rest of their lives."

It would not have been surprising if the children had emerged speaking English, for that language seems completely naturalized in India, as the works of Salman Rushdie, Arundhati Roy, Vikram Chandra, Vikram Seth, and a good many others would suggest.

No part of English culture has better fit the Indian soul, though, than Shakespeare. An early and wonderful Merchant and Ivory film is called *Shakespeare Wallah,* and it is about the Kendrick family of actors in post-Independence India, who toured performing nothing but Shakespeare. And just a few years ago I had the pleasure of accompanying my friend David Grene while he addressed The Shakespeare Society in Calcutta, and variations of it in other cities, and was as astonished as David was, not so much at the erudition in Shakespearean writing and lore displayed as at the completeness of permeation of the intellectual lives of those concerned: the

most ordinary conversation is laced with obscure references to *Timon of Athens* and *Pericles*.

It is particularly astonishing because Manu talks about
actors in the same sentence in which he mentions ghouls
and ogres. He says that you can't take food from an actor,
any more than you can from an arms dealer, without becoming polluted. I wonder if that means that you can't
take food *with* one, for the only time I have ever broken
bread with an actor was in Clark's Hotel in Agra in 1961.
It was the only decent hotel that Agra had, then, and,
therefore, the only decent restaurant. It was customary
in those family-oriented days, if the restaurant was
crowded, or even if it was empty and the waiter didn't
want to walk any farther than he had to, to seat other
people at your table without so much as a by-your-leave.

I had given a lecture at the university that afternoon,
was tired, and was eating an early dinner in an empty
restaurant at a table set with four places. I looked up
from my chicken curry to see the waiter seating a gentleman diagonally opposite me. I thought he looked familiar, but no bells started ringing, so we nodded to each
other, made some innocuous remarks about the beauty
of the Taj Mahal, which he had come to see, and, wiping
away tears of pain, set about cleansing our sinuses with
the curry.

He finished before I did, excused himself, and made a

dignified exit. I called the waiter over and asked him if he knew the gentleman's name. "Oh, yes," he said, "oh yes. That is the American movie actor, Mr. Edward G. Robinson." I would have known him in an instant if only he had said to me out of the side of his mouth, "Shut up, see, and listen, or my yeggs'll wipe the floor with ya, see?" But he didn't.

Though Manu doesn't care for actors, that doesn't mean that others do not revere them. In fact, in some places the child actors playing Radha and Krishna are honored and worshiped just as if they were the real thing (just as in places in Europe people playing parts in Nativity tableaux, or playing the crucified Jesus, are considered holy, at least for a while, and as, in an earlier and simpler time, people in this country threw things at the villains on the silver screen, sometimes hitting Fatty Arbuckle by mistake). In fact, you are almost forced to admire actors in India. Some friends of ours once took us to a performance by a local repertory company. I don't know to this day what it was they were, and perhaps still are, performing, for I remember little of it, except that the play began at nine, and when we left at midnight they were still in the prologue. I also remember that all during this prologue people in the audience kept jumping up and running up to the stage shouting things like "Louder!" or "That was a stupid thing to say!" or "You have mustard on your shirt!", while other members of the audience chatted with one another, voices raised to be heard above the din, about the price of milk. In other words, the audience was just participating in the unruly joyful hubbub that is India, while the actors, also participating, just kept doing their thing.

It is even that way, I should hasten to point out, at some Hindu religious services. Far from the austere solemnity that characterizes the holy places and times of some other religions, the temple that you enter will have many deities all in their own niches, each with his or her small or large congregations, depending on the occasion, and his or her own priests zestily intoning away from a variety of texts and waving lights, and music will be playing and gongs will be gonging and bells ringing and and people circumambulating around and offering flowers and taking holy water to sip and put on their heads and generally enjoying themselves (though none of this means that the purpose is not serious). A Hindu friend told me once that he had seen a temple, following its dedication ceremony, that looked like a hurricane had passed through, or like Wrigley Field after a Cubs game: empty coke bottles were everywhere, chairs had been taken from their orderly rows and arranged in haphazard groups, there was litter all about; the place generally looked like people had been there having a wonderful time. For all I know, that may be just the way God likes it. Manu, though, would be a little distressed.

The Calf Finds Its Mother

*In which the author encounters karma
and its complications.*

Playing golf in India is, in its essentials, not very different from playing golf elsewhere. There are, of course, minor differences: little temples and tombs of saints in the middle of the fairways, cobras in the rough, and I am told that if you overshoot the ninth green on the "highest golf course in the world," in Darjeeling, your ball plunges four hundred feet into a clear glacial stream that carries it to Bangladesh. Many mulligans are taken. What is different, in India, is that it is on the golf course that some of the clearest demonstrations of the law of karma are to be found.

Karma as a principle of golf is not unknown elsewhere, of course. In fact, what is known in some golfing circles as The Shot was made on the course at Cummaquid, on Cape Cod, before that comfortably brown and sandy place had become green and bloated to twice its normal size and had acquired a regular clubhouse to replace the pockmarked shack that had sheltered the beer cooler and the man who collected the three-dollar greens fees. The ball lay an easy eight-iron from the pin, but I got up on it a bit too much, hit it in the middle, and sent it, about three feet off the ground, on a line right over the "green" at the top of the rise on which my ball lay. My despairing cry at this turn of events was cut short by a metallic clang, as what to my wondering eyes should appear but my ball, making a high arc and coming back to rest about two feet from the pin. It had hit the hood of a tractor pulling a grass cutter just out of sight over the rise, no doubt surprising not only the groundskeeper but also my three companions, who could not keep from expressing their admiration. "Lucky son of a bitch" is one of the comments that sticks in my mind. But, as we are all aware that golfers can be small-minded and jealous people, we should not allow such comments to wound. I, at least, am certain that luck had nothing at all to do with it. The whole episode was the result of my having done some minor good deed in a former life. Had I done a major good deed, like giving a cow to a Brahman, the ball would have gone into the cup.

There are many misconceptions about India held by people in the West: that the temples there are filled with idols with ruby eyes, that Elvis is living in a cave in the

Himalayas and, most significant, that their belief in the doctrine of karma causes the people of that country to sit around staring into the middle distance awaiting the fate they cannot escape. In fact, a good deal of activity is necessary in order to go about even the most mundane of chores, such as crossing the street. The only thing that causes your average Indian driver to deviate from his bullet-straight path is a cow. Other life forms—pedestrians, rickshaw pullers, dogs, camels, bicyclists, the whole variety that occupies Indian roads—must fend for themselves, leaping out of the way with acrobatic agility, or in some more macho cases merely moving their hips slightly in a bullfighter's pirouette to show contempt for the horn of the metallic monster passing at great speed two inches from their asses. The driver of your car has equal faith in his own abilities and in the goodwill and sense of his fellow man. He will pass an overburdened and seriously listing truck at sixty miles per hour on a two-lane shoulderless road merely on the strength of the minute movement of the truck driver's hand, which is hanging out the window on the end of a limp wrist, a gesture that always looks to me like he is waving a casual hello to a distant relative or acquaintance on the side of the road. Once in a while, of course, he will actually be waving to an acquaintance, and in that case your karma matters rather a lot.

It is difficult to believe, therefore, that all Indian drivers and pedestrians were not, in previous existences, bats. I mean to say, they are bats now, but in previous existences they were used to hurtling toward one another at terrific speeds in the dark, navigating by sonar and blind faith. Driving at night in Calcutta has something of the same feel about it. When the system breaks down, the result is catastrophic, but between those times things run with an extraordinary efficiency and a good deal of cheery dependence of individuals each upon the other.

One of the mysteries of the universe is that in the rest of the universe, repetition of an act seems to enhance the chance of a negative result, while in sports it does not. This is another way in which sports are removed from reality. For example, the more times you assume that the spasmodic movement of the truck driver's hand is intentional and not the result of a nervous tic or a cousin by the roadside, the higher the chances will be that you will be mistaken. On the other hand, the more times you swing at a golf ball (those were practice swings), the better the chances should be that when you do hit it you will do it right. Practice lessens the chance of accident, or so we are told, and thus it is more of a shock when accident occurs. As with any structure, it is the offbeat that gets your attention. We are told that possibilities are concentrated by some force that we do not understand to become probabilities, and probabilities are concentrated to become events. If things have gone right for you, for instance, you may find yourself, as you read this, sitting at your desk or comfortably in your easy chair, and not paying good money to go on a dog-sled expedition to Cornwallis Island. Practice swings are possibilities. Enough of them and you hit the ball. Enough hits and you get it right, and onward and upward to perfection, as we used to say in the nineteenth century. It also helps if your past lives have been beyond reproach.

But no scheme, of course, is entirely without flaws. In the real world, the professional gets the perfect stroke more than chance would allow, but occasionally blows it, striking out with the bases loaded or slicing one into the standing water that ends up on the alligator's nose. The duffer gets the perfect stroke very rarely, but often gets it the first time he swings, thus hooking him on the game for life (if you listen carefully you can sometimes hear the golf fairies tittering in the bushes behind the first tee). The fact is that practice never makes perfect, except perhaps in infinite amounts, and few of us have time for that. In the meantime, on the advanced level at least, such practice brings in *mucho* bucks.

The theological part of the question, of course, is that of causation: What made God in the first place tee off with the Big Bang, getting too much wrist into it and slicing it into the rough? As David Hume has shown us, even God is not perfect, though he has had plenty of time to practice. What caused that concentration of possibilities? Well, I can't answer that. It is a question that has bothered many people in different times and places, though, so you need not feel alone. It is possible that the answer is simpler, and thus more elegant, than we now think. God may have been more than usually irritated that morning. Some of his favorite people are known to be. For example, the prophet Elijah, we are told in II Kings, had forty-two children eaten by she-bears because they made fun of his bald head. We seek the Freudian explanation (i.e., the story represents an inversion of the Oedipal impulse) or the Christian one (i.e., the kids were born in sin, and it served them damn well right), but it is quite possible that Elijah was simply pissed off. Perhaps it is wisdom that makes one irritable, for Elijah shares his irascibility with another wise person, namely, the sage Vishvamitra, "Everybody's Friend," who, it may be remembered, once grumpily caused the virtuous and noble king Harischandra to suffer horribly in this life and others because the king had neglected to wish him a good morning. Or maybe Elijah and Vishvamitra were only being human. The other day, as I was walking my dog, Nikki, early in the morning, as is my wont, I passed my ordinarily cheerful neighbor and said "Good morning" to him, as I always do. "Oh, go to hell, George," he replied, using the name he applies to everyone indiscriminately, and making me aware once again that one can easily get out of the wrong side of the bed, some days, and step in the cat's hairball. Or, as a Hindu might say, perhaps a demon had eaten his good nature that morning.

This is the kind of attitude that makes Hindus extraordinarily easy folk to live among. Some of it may be just plain niceness, though having pity for stones may seem to some a little oversensitive. Once you grant the possibility that these stones may be someone you know, though, life takes on a different cast, and the world in general seems more intimate. The rocks in your garden may even be relatives, for they are there again even though you cleaned them all out last spring.

Hindus traditionally not only explain the blips in the graph line of social tranquillity with charity, but courteously hold that the uglier tendencies of people must be attributable to previous births. "The calf," say some Hindu thinkers, perhaps a trifle smugly, "finds its mother," if not in this birth, then in some other one.

Some of the connections made in this way, while perhaps obvious to others, seem to me quite tenuous. It is said, for example, that if you adulterate grain you will grow redundant limbs, and if you destroy a park you will be stricken with dysentery (I tried to explain this to the kids who were leaving chicken bones and beer cans all over the park down the street, and tearing all reachable limbs off the flowering trees, but they felt, as does all youth, beyond the reach of such consequences). Other connections seem a little clearer. We are told by Manu and many of the other books of instruction on the matter, for instance, that drinking wine assures one of a birth as an ass (overloaded, braying, long-eared but gentle, stubborn, having no warts on its hind legs, and sharing with the camel an aversion to running water, a fact to which I am sure we shall have occasion to return).

When you begin to think in these patterns, all sorts of things begin to make sense: MVPs in the American League must return as Little Sisters of the Poor, Roland Barthes as the primary character in a hypertext novel, those with the burden of arrogance as identical twins, and so on. Or, if you choose, you can reason deductively: a person has bad breath because that person has told lies about another.

This view of time, among other things, allows Hindus to preserve their intellectual balance and to avoid the asymmetry between past and future that is so troublesome to some other religions. It must be said, however, that before you conclude that here is a system in which justice is absolute and impeccable, you should realize that if it were so I would at this moment be leaning back on the Divan of Hafiz smelling roses.

Before we move on to discuss the general types of sins that cause unhappiness in present and future lives, I might just mention a question that has bothered Buddhists for a long time: What is it that carries the cause-

and-effect connection? It is certainly not the physical form, for it is likely that your cousin looks different from the rock in your garden; on the other hand, both may exhibit the same type of animation (to Hindus, rocks and trees are animate but take their own sweet time about things). It may be, instead, quality that provides the connection.

The Dharma-Shastras observe that there are three general types of sins. The first is the bodily type, and the favorite example of it, here and elsewhere, is adultery. The result of adultery is that you come back as a fixed object such as a stone or a tree stump, and you can see by the number of stones and stumps around that there has been a lot of this going on. The result of incest is that you come back as grass. The second type of sin is mental, which is a very modern position. Members of the lowest castes are here because of such sins, and if I were writing these Dharma-Shastras, I should place in this category plump-cheeked movie actors with thin mustaches. And the third category comprises those sins known as "vocal," including "irrelevant prattling." I will stonily ignore the obvious, and I would appreciate it if you would, too, and be content with the observation that if one commits one of these sins one comes back as a beast or a bird, perhaps a bluejay or a rap singer, or the donkey or ass we spoke of before.

The ass was, despite all its excellent qualities, hated

by the Egyptians, but their opinion can be safely ignored because they were partial to beetles.

Or, maybe, you might get to be a camel. While it shares with the ass an aversion to running water, the camel is not nearly as cute (though it does have big old soft, flexible feet). A camel is what you get to be not only for vocal sins, but for the theft of a vehicle. I do not doubt for an instant that this is true, for in addition to its lip-curling scorn for ordinary civility, the camel is an ungainly and stupid beast, and it also steals things other than vehicles. One of them once snatched a favorite hat of mine (a dashing wide-brimmed job of the ANZAC variety) right off my head as I was walking along a street in Port Said minding my own business. It (the camel) had that smug, defiant, arrogant, sly look that you often see on car thieves. In sum, it is possible to say that camels are very unlike their sweet-natured cousins the llamas, except that they both spit when they are mad, or when they are meditating, like baseball managers.

So your question probably is, What will we do with all this information? We can be of good cheer, for according to how we behave in this life, our eternity is eventually assured. Furthermore, we have been provided with omens to help us out in situations of ambiguity or when responsibility for making a decision is simply too great. The *tiktiki,* the little gecko lizard that lives quietly behind the Jamini Roy painting on your wall, not only pays his rent and more by eating all the bugs (or perhaps they are relatives) he can get his flickering little tongue on but will demonstrate his proprietary feeling for you by telling you, with a clicking noise, whether you should go out or not. And in addition to such specific provisions, there are more general ones to ensure your welfare. As in my part of the world one does not undertake a voyage on a Friday, that being the day of the Crucifixion (its malevolent power being multiplied when it coincides with the number of people at the Last Supper), so, in India, Saturday is not considered the best day. Saturday, there as well as here, is considered to be under the influence of the troublesome planet Saturn and therefore is thoroughly rotten news. Saturn is related astrologically to the god Sani, who is, among other things, responsible for baldness, and if he had known that, Elijah might have chilled out a little. Sani is also connected to grief, the West, eunuchs, astringency, crime, and discipline, so you can see what fun Saturday is ("the loneliest night of the week," according to a recent poet). It has the power to bring about untold misery and suffering. Sani's mother, in mythology, was a shadow, so what do you expect?

Anyway, there are signs that help you avoid the places where the possibilities of disaster are densest. Mongooses, which are basically creepy, ferretlike creatures with very sharp teeth, have little to recommend them aesthetically, but they share with most of the rest of us an intense dislike of poisonous snakes, and are considered lucky. Deer are also signs of good luck, when they appear to your right-hand side. And furthermore, if you do happen to stagger to the starboard and step in the deer-doo, there are penances you can perform to help you get it off your shoe. If you have intercourse in a cart drawn by oxen, for instance, you can rid yourself of all stigma attached to that by bathing in your clothes.

Some foods are forbidden (or "naughty") by their nature. These are called *svabhavadushta,* if you really want to know, and include garlic and leeks—and to the list I should like to add broccoli and Jerusalem artichokes. Before you panic, though, you should know that Manu considered the eating of forbidden foods only a little crime, in the same category as having sex with a woman who drinks wine or professing atheism. To purify yourself, you need only fast for a day, which probably wouldn't hurt, anyway.

How to Succeed in Business

*In which the author is given a ride
on an elephant.*

Manu says in the same sentence that trade is both "good" and "unlawful." I think that he is not just being difficult, but that he feels fairly strongly that trade is, for a priest, degrading, but for everybody else, perfectly okay; he understands that everybody has to make a living (on the whole, I get the feeling that he'd rather you be a priest, though). He realizes that India cannot be populated entirely by bearded folk with sad but piercing eyes, along the lines of the Maharishi Maheshyogi.

Some years ago, I remember seeing in the newspaper, the Maharishi wanted to negotiate a contract with the City of Chicago, under the terms of which, at a cost of 111 million dollars only, he would eliminate crime from the city. "For a city of six million," the Maharishi was quoted as saying, "where the police is taking billions, no one would even count." Inset into the column was a picture of the Maharishi, looking benign and somewhat wistful behind his long salt-and-pepper beard, withdrawn from the world, as ascetics are supposed to be while they are devising imaginative financial schemes. The plan was to bring in "three thousand top-of-the-line meditators," the power of whose thought would bring order out of the existing chaos. "The program itself has no charge," the Maharishi was quoted as saying, "but there are expenses."

An idea that runs throughout Hindu texts is that thinking generates heat (the top of your head eventually blows off, just like a volcano), and thinking combined with asceticism generates such power that changes in the environment are brought about in a hurry, and you can bend the world to your will (Vishvamitra, "Everybody's Friend," didn't get to where he is by the sweetness of his smile, you know). So the Maharishi, in seeking to trade thinking for money, is well within the Hindu tradition. Thinking as commercial property is a notion familiar to this culture, too, sometimes at universities. The concept feels more familiar if we think of the Maharishi as a kind of offbeat-looking Presbyterian, for whom the acquisition of immense wealth is but proof of his favor in God's eyes; as it was to Andrew Carnegie, it is a sign that he has done properly and well. It is also true in the Hindu tradition, it may surprise some to learn (despite Manu's ambivalence), that the acquisition of wealth is one of life's principal aims (together with erotic enjoyment, righteousness, and the ultimate realization that none of the above are worth anything).

The gaining of access to wealth and power is the subject of a good many "how-to" books of the classical Indian tradition, books collectively called the *Arthashastra.* The wealth consists of education (listen up, Washington), land, cattle, corn, domestic utensils, political clout, and, of course, money. This was, some thirty or forty centuries ago, a fairly forward-looking list, and, except perhaps for domestic utensils and corn, with which we are tolerably well supplied, the items are still much in demand. We could all use more of them.

Just how you go about gaining this wealth and power, the *Arthashastra* leaves reasonably wide open. If you are a Brahman you can sell all the grass (in its old sense) or wool that you care to, though not if it is far away (eliminating that nice piece of property in Arizona). You cannot, however, sell pools, pleasure gardens, wives or children, stones, salt, livestock, animals with fangs or horns, or ever, under any circumstances, birds. Apart from this, it is pretty much what the traffic will bear. As for methods, one text tells us that you "should be courteous in speech, but have a heart like a razor." In another, a sage advises that "one desirous of property should fold one's hands, take an oath, use sweet words, place his

head at another's feet, shed tears, . . . and when a fit opportunity arises, one should break [the object of all this
attention] like an earthen pot upon a stone." To get the
full effect of this attention-grabbing figure, you should
realize that after you have eaten or drunk from an earth-
enware pot, you are to smash it, thus promoting hygiene
and keeping both potters and archeologists doing a lively
business.

So the world of trade and commerce would be a
pretty cutthroat one if it were not for the regulations that
enjoin courtesy and such. As it is elsewhere in the world,
where there is latitude it is quickly filled up by people
staking their various claims. Although Brahmans are not
supposed to sell stones, in the New Market in Calcutta
you will not have to wander far before coming across a
Brahman selling rubies, who will tell you that the regulation is referring to paving stones. It is always of interest
to me to observe, on the faces of people who have just
parked their cars under No Parking signs, expressions
either of blank incomprehension or of the ecstasy that
comes from direct and immediate communication with
God, or from trade in the illicit grass we have spoken of
before.

You can get anything in that market, including wild
animals, which Brahmans are also not supposed to sell.
When my family and I lived in Chowringhee Lane, just
around the corner from the market, my little daughter

would often tease me, early in the morning, until I walked with her to the market so that she could play with the tiger cubs and other small creatures in the casual, though I am sorry to say cruelly unsanitary, places in which they were kept, while their owners would ineffectually try to sell me a twelve-foot python.

The larger animals, the adult tigers and elephants and so on, were for reasons of law and also common sense kept outside of the city, and once a year, in the neighboring state of Bihar, an elephant fair would be held. To this fair buyers from all over the world would come and buy elephants (and, often, necessarily, their accompanying mahouts and small friends such as caged guinea pigs, to whom the elephants were much attached and without whose calming presence they would tend to become obstreperous) for zoos at Teheran or Adelaide, or for work in Thailand or in the teak forests of the Malabar Coast. At one point in time, Bengal did a fairly lively commerce in elephants, and some sixteenth-century texts speak of shiploads of them on their way to Sri Lanka. One was also sent to Pope Leo X, who must have had a fondness for huge beasts—you might recall that a group of thoughtful admirers had also sent Leo a rhinoceros, which was unfortunately drowned in a shipwreck; his gift elephant was a good deal luckier, and also more popular, and made a great hit, bowing three times to the pope and then squirting water all over the assembled cardinals, the big imp.

The word *elephant* is first used by Herodotus to mean the whole animal (Homer and Hesiod had also used the word, but to refer to the tusks only). The form the word takes in Old Swedish seems to be *ulbandus,* which, however, also means "camel." One can understand why Old Swedes, not knowing much about either elephants or camels, might have confused the two. But one would expect something different from Pathans, who, while not always cosmopolitan in the best sense of the word, do live in the same general neighborhood as elephants. Yet there is a story that in the 1860s, when a British force was proceeding through Pathan territory with their elephants in train, one of the Pathan village women who had gathered to watch the passage of the exotic group asked a trooper of the Frontier Horse what the great gray things were. "Why," he replied, "those are the queen's buffaloes. Imgaine how much milk they give."

Swedes and Pathans aside, an elephant is an elephant, and anyone who has driven on the Delhi-Agra road and come spinning around a corner under a railway bridge and face-to-face (so to speak) with an elephant's rear end twenty-five feet away will know what I mean. Actually, if you have time to admire it, an elephant's rear end is most graceful, or at least the way the elephant moves it is; in fact, the better Sanskrit poets compare it favorably to the swaying walk of a perfect-postured, full-hipped woman. And the thing is, these elephants are as deliberate and careful in their walk as they are elegant. If you'll come to Benares with me for a little while, we'll take a ride on one.

Actually, we'll go to Benares and then across the Ganges River, to a place called Ramnagar, where the biggest of the big festivals is held each year. It is called the Ram-lila, and it is the enactment of the long and complicated story of how the divine hero Rama and his wife Sita and his allies the monkeys and his enemies the antigods all get embroiled in the struggle between good and evil (in Bengal, which can be a perverse place, the antigods are sometimes seen as the heroes, and Rama as something of a self-satisfied wimp). The stage is the whole town, and the audience, a great mob of people from all over India, moves from location to location as the action shifts. Thus the best seat in the house is both itinerant and high; it is, in other words, the back of an elephant.

The elephant who provided me this seat was named Gopal, and he, and several others of his kind, belonged to the Maharaja of Benares. It happened that the American Institute of Indian Studies, upon whose business I found myself in Benares, was renting one of the maharaja's more magnificent buildings to house part of its library. A most courteous landlord and gentleman, the maharaja would every year at the time of Ram-lila send one or two of his elephants to transport those who were interested in seeing the drama. Gopal knelt politely and with the great patience of his kind in the courtyard at the foot of the library steps. I had never before had the opportunity to look into an elephant's eye, being of average height, but as I passed Gopal's head to mount the short ladder that led to the howdah on his back, I had what came close to a shock. In my experience, most animals' eyes register generalized emotions—anger, contentment, even playfulness—but Gopal's eye showed intelligence, a sad wisdom, a kind of mild curiosity, and a knowing humor that I have come to associate with older people who have seen a good deal of life and loved some of it and hated some of it but don't want to talk about any of it anymore. The elephant seemed very much, in fact, like my father.

Anyway, when we were settled, Gopal rose and swayed off through the crowds, although the people seated on the ground were so densely packed that you wouldn't have thought there was room for his great foot. But each step was high, and he made sure that before he started the downward motion, the person beneath had had time to look up, sometimes call a greeting, and move enough to one side so that the foot could come gently down. Although elephants were used as tanks in war, and by some Mughal emperors as a means of execution of criminals, I cannot believe that they enjoyed such ferocity; they wanted to please their people.

So you can't buy your elephant in the New Market, but in addition to the pythons and tiger cubs, there are lots of birds, the enemies of their own freedom because of the beauty of their plumage or their ability, however limited, to carry on a conversation in some human language. Brahmans are forbidden to sell them also, but Indian classical dramatists and poets were charmed not only by the gait of elephants but by the counterfeit intelligence of parrots and mynah birds, and these birds play sometimes significant roles in drama. Much like a Greek chorus (literally, in Aristophanes' *The Birds*), they will sit there on their perches and make obvious or irrelevant remarks, and once in a while pickily observe or suggest something that changes the course of the drama abruptly. A hero might be tied to the stake in the execution ground, for instance, with the king about to pass the death sentence, when one bird perched in a tree will say to another, "Mraaak! The stupid defense attorney doesn't know what we know, that it was his brother-in-law who slipped the gunpowder into the chicken curry."

Sometimes, therefore, the birds are eaten by villains, sold to them by other villains who have caught them in a net or shot them with arrows. Trade is trade. And with the irony that pervades Indian mythology and literature, the story goes that the sage Valmiki, legendary author of the epic *Ramayana,* seeing a hunter kill the male of an inseparable pair of birds, cursed that hunter in a wonderful new meter; so a curse made possible the most complex and beautiful of Sanskrit poetry.

The Snake Catcher Knows How the Serpent Sneezes

In which the author and his children
meet the gilli-gilli *man.*

Once you have met a maharaja, ridden on an elephant, and seen a ruby-eyed idol, all that remains for you to do in order to say that you have really seen India is find a cobra. This task, while more difficult than one would be led to believe by the popular press, is by no means impossible. But the fact is that in some parts of India these fearsome, irritable creatures have been reduced from the status of plague to one of inconvenience, and the people of those areas look upon them much as they look upon the often-substantial mosquitoes.

Cobra is a Portuguese word derived from the Latin *colubra,* a generic word for snakes. The Portuguese felt a pressing need to be more specific, for in India they had run into a creature that, when irritated, puts on a kind of monk's hood, or *capelo,* and a pair of glasses (perhaps to see who is annoying it). So they called it a *cobra de capelo,* which seemed to satisfy everybody except perhaps those monks who wore little glasses down on the ends of their noses, like Benjamin Franklin.

It is a common misconception that cobras flourish in India because the people there are generally inclined toward peaceful coexistence. The fact of the matter is much more complicated, and I have known a good many Indians who are quite as ready as the next person to smack the nearest cobra upside the head. It is of course true that there are many who do feel that cobras have a right to their share of God's green or brown earth, and a subgroup of these who think that it is not at all an unfair exchange to have a animated rattrap living quietly in the thatched roof of the granary, and will even leave it a cup of warm milk to sip before retiring. The relationship is complicated for many reasons, including the fact that the god Shiva, who is strange in many ways, wears cobras in his hair. This makes it difficult to comb, but Shiva doesn't care about that any more than Medusa does, and perhaps less. Another reason why Indians react in interesting ways to these cobras involves aesthetics.

I was once, in the mid-1960s, staying with a friend in a remote village in Bengal, and we were out one afternoon for a stroll on a path in the jungle (which in that part of the world implies not a green, impenetrable place with lianas draped from huge trees, but a wasteland more sparse and brown). As we rounded a bend in the path, there in front of us was a huge cobra, Dominican in color, with light-brown spectacles, rearing itself up. My companion threw his arm across my chest to stop any further progress (he needn't have, for I had already turned to stone) and exhaled in a long, slow whistle. I, of course, assumed that he was as petrified as I, but he whispered in awe, "Isn't he beautiful!" The snake, after swaying there in bravado for a little while, clearly reasoned that when I had recovered my usual aplomb I would bruise his head, and finally decided that discretion was the better part of valor and made his way in a dignified fashion into the bush.

I had a similar experience a few years later when I found myself aboard a leaky but character-filled (in more ways than one) wooden fishing boat, a dragger named *St. Lawrence,* out of Goa, as a kind of supercargo. In other words, I had been hanging around the waterfront for some days, watching the boats come and go, with the pitiful look of a landbound sailor in my eyes and carriage. The skipper of the St. Lawrence, taking in with a single, shrewd glance both the tongue hanging out of my mouth and the hundred-rupee note hanging out of my pocket, suggested that perhaps my friend and I would like to join his ship's complement the next day. We had done so, and I was thoroughly enjoying it, sitting on the cabin top as the boat rocked in a gentle swell, savoring a cool bottle of Golden Eagle and watching the sleds come up from the bottom, their nets filled with not only shrimp but all sorts of other exotically colored creatures of the sea, which were for the most part thrown back unceremoniously. After the second or third drag, one of the crewmen reached into the writhing tangle of marine life and pulled out of it a four-foot snake, a multicolored specimen, which he grasped by what I suppose might be called its neck, and held it out to me so that I could examine its gaudy colors at closer range. I was of course aware that snakes in the Arabian Sea can be more venomous than those in any other part of the world. I assured my enthusiastic shipmate that I could see quite as well from the rigging, which is where I now found myself, as from closer in. His disappointment at my lack of appreciation was palpable, but he seemed to accept my detailed explanation (though he spoke no English or Hindi, and I no Konkani) that my taste ran to less gaudy colors, and that a snake in a subdued taupe with perhaps charcoal highlights would be more in my line, so he reluctantly threw the creature back over the side.

Cobras, as I've said, are irritable creatures, somewhat on the order of Vishvamitra or Elijah. Hindus see that this irascibility sometimes works to human benefit. For one thing, it causes the cobras to eat their young ("If you don't stop whining about the toy store, I'll have you for dinner"), and as the folktales of India tell us, if they did not eat their young we would shortly be up to our hunkies in cobras. Another reason for Hindu tolerance of cobras is that Hindus understand how their irritability came about and do not blame the snakes at all.

There are three historical explanations for this irritability. The first is buried in the mists of time. It seems that there was a gentle king named Parikshit, who, as a reward for minding his own business, was bitten by a cobra named Takshaka. This was accomplished by disguising a lot of snakes as Brahmans, while Takshaka himself became a worm and hid in an apple, along with a lot of other entertaining goings-on of that nature. The upshot of it all was that a great king named Janamejaya, the Saint Patrick of India (failed), decided to eradicate these snakes, which had become a nuisance to all, by urging them with irresistible mantras to wriggle their way into a sacrificial fire. An accommodation was worked out, but the misfire has made snakes a little jumpy ever since.

The second reason for the irritability of cobras has to do with a very large snake named Kaliya, who was unusual in that he had a thousand heads. In other repects he was fairly normal. For example, he poisoned the river in which he lived, just like your run-of-the-mill fertilizer factory. He got his, though, for polluting the environment. When the cowherd god Krishna came down to the river one day with all his friends and cows, the cowherds took a drink of the river water and fell down dead. Krishna, in retaliation, began to dance on one of Kaliya's heads, and he kept it up until Kaliya agreed to move out of the neighborhood. I happen to know exactly how he felt, having lived in downstairs apartments. One can only wish that the solution to the problem of fertilizer factories were as straightforward.

Yet a third reason has to do with the phenomenon known as the *gilli-gilli* man. I can best introduce him to you by describing how, occasionally, of a morning in Calcutta, my children, on the balcony from which they habitually watched with interest the varied life of the street before going down to join it, would begin to give little jumps and squeals of anticipation. Then there would come the sound of the great big-band drummer Gene Krupa doing a five-minute paradiddle with accented sixteenths. This announced the *gilli-gilli* man, who carried in one hand, like Shiva, a little two-headed, hourglass-shaped drum; the rapid movement of his wrist would make the two knots tied to the drum strike the opposite heads with tricky syncopated rhythms. In his other hand he carried a burlap bag full of snakes. These snakes, in reponse to the small coins that my children cadged and tossed over the balcony railing, performed tricks. One of the tricks they performed was to disappear, which delighted the children no end, and bemused me not a little as well. The *gilli-gilli* man would collect his cobras into the bag, mutter some magic words (*gilli-gilli*) over them, and slam the bag with all his might against the wall of the house. When he shook the bag, there would be no snakes in it. And then, after a certain amount more conversation, he would slam it again, and the snakes would reappear. In the meantime, to keep up the suspense, he would stick swords into a big basket that contained his wife. You might think that there was some kind of sleight-of-hand involved, but you were not there, and my children and I knew that we had witnessed something profound. The point in question here, however, is that being slammed against concrete walls does little to add to the snakes' good nature.

The *gilli-gilli* man, of course, preserved the ecological equilibrium by sending away and bringing back the same number of snakes, but in case you are wondering how the snakes, being generally reclusive creatures and content to mind their own business, are brought into contact with the irritating human environment in the first place, there is a story about a certain "High German" (it goes without saying) known as "The Snake Catcher." This man was summoned, the story goes, to catch a "Cobra Capel" that was making a nuisance of itself. The man did it, merely holding his hat before his eyes and seizing the snake with his hand, without any damage. I don't know how, or even whether, serpents sneeze, but if they do, this man would know about it as the proverb says he might.

There is in fact a great deal of lore about people who seem to have no fear at all of snakes, and who in fact take seriously the word of Genesis, in which God says to the serpent: "And I will put enmity between thee and the woman, and between thy seed and her seed; it shall bruise thy head, and thou shalt bruise his heel." One such true seed of Eve, otherwise anonymous, advises us in a book called *Tribes on My Frontier* to do as he does and carry with us in our walks abroad a strong, supple walking cane. "Armed with it, you may rout and slaughter the hottest-tempered cobra in Hindustan. Let it rear itself up and bluster as it will; but one rap on the side of its head will bring it to reason." One can almost hear his triumphant cry of "Take that, four-eyes!" What constitutes reason in this situation can perhaps safely be left undiscussed.

B Natural

In which the author surfs the unhearing winds.

It is sometimes forgotten that the Sanskritic languages are distant cousins to the European ones, and that a degree of family resemblance remains despite some generations of living and breeding apart. This resemblance sometimes shows up in cognate words and in similarities among the concepts carried by the two sets of languages. One such concept is that of nature. In each set, *nature* seems to signify both the raw stuff of creation and "that which is," the quality that gives a thing its distinctiveness from other parts of the whole. In the Latinate languages, the stem is that of *nation* and *nativity,* which suggests birth in the world and participation by an individual in an organism, an ecosystem, even, perhaps, a family. The Sanskritic languages have the stem *ja-*, meaning about the same thing.

Rudyard Kipling once made a remark, which I have heard repeated by others, to the effect that East and West are separate and will not meet. Kipling, of course, cannot be blamed for his shortsightedness, for he lived at a time when people in India were sensible and would hang in their doorways and windows what were, and perhaps in some obscure corners still are, called *tattis*. These *tattis* were thick mats woven from fragrant grasses, and in the hot season every once in a while a man would come along and throw buckets of water on them, and when the breeze blew through them the house would be cool and sweet-smelling. This was a time-honored and altogether exceptional way to beat the heat, although perhaps on the twentieth floor of an office building it might be somewhat impractical. In any case, it turns out upon further review that most Indians are not meant to live in India, for not only is the curry too hot for them, but they would be far more comfortable on the shores of Baffin Bay, as demonstrated by the fact that they have adopted, with a vengeance, a Western aberration called "air-conditioning." One might argue that this only indicates participation in a world that is constantly in flux, or one might argue that these Indians have adopted a tense, Western-style hostility toward nature. For the moment, I shall be satisfied with pointing out that for one who wears glasses, time spent in moving periodically between environments that are 55 degrees on the one hand and 110 on the other is time spent, often unsuccessfully, trying to avoid bumping into stationary objects.

I must say that I understand the problem, at least better than I understand the solution. In April and May the heat in Calcutta, for example, is perfectly incredible, and the humidity worse than that. If you have the good fortune to live in a building where you can go up on a reasonably high roof, you might find a breeze. Closer to the street, the air solidifies. Ceiling fans muscle it around a little bit and make a mess of your papers if they are not weighted down with brass objects or blobs of glass or cups of tea or heavy books. Despite the fans, unless you keep your head way back, which makes it difficult to see what you are writing, the sweat drips from your brow or from the end of your nose and blurs the ink; the paper is anyway already soggy from the sweat of your forearm. In other words, until God comes along and throws the bucket of water, which he usually does along about June, it is quite uncomfortable.

As God likes to tease, he does not throw the whole bucket at once. In Baishakh, which is the month that begins in what we think of as the middle of May, you will be sitting there dripping onto your notes and thinking fuzzily about tall, cool things, when all of a sudden, as Alexander Frater describes it in his excellent book *Chasing the Monsoon,* "the sun goes out and a bomb goes off a hundred feet above your head"; the wooden shutters begin to clatter as if some clog dancers were warming up in the room right above you, and those experienced with the matter begin to dash about trying to get everything battened down before more than an inch of water gets onto the floor. But in a few minutes the skies will be clear again, and it will be as hot as it was before, only muggier. These brief, ferocious storms are called Kal Baishakhi, and the premonsoon period that spawns them is a difficult one in the city. In the countryside they have what is known as "the brain-fever bird" *(avis infernalis)* to help you through the nights. This bird starts its song on a C and goes up the scale, sounding each note as if it were an instrument string being tightened or a person whistling for his dog, until it reaches A. It then goes to B flat, back down to C, and starts all over again. This is designed to catch tempers at just the right degree of shortness, and, if the community happens to be a multilingual one, you can usually hear from all directions hoarse voices in different languages requesting the bird to "Finish the goddamn octave and shut the hell up!" or offering variations on that theme. So one of the nice things about living in the city is that sometimes you have three or four straight hours when the only sound to be heard, apart from the hawking and spitting and snoring, is the desultory clunk of a rickshaw puller's bell.

After a month or so of this, if God chooses to be kind,

as he does more often than not, it begins to rain in earnest, and people rejoice at the coming of the monsoon. "In earnest" means that walls of water fall from the sky. As hyperbolic as it may seem to someone who has not experienced it, the scene in Satyajit Ray's film of Bibhutibhushan Banerji's novel *Pather Panchali,* in which the children run out into the first rains with their faces uplifted and transformed with joy, is precisely the paradigm. Everything, people included, bursts into life. Leaves and flowers appear from the dust, literally overnight. In the drier parts of India, before the rain, the earth is cracked like a vast dull ochre mosaic and hard as concrete, and it seems impossible that anything can be alive in it. But frogs and fish that were not there before are there now, and some people believe, as I do, that these creatures fall with the rain. The *chataka* bird *(cucculus melanoleucus)* who, the poets say, gets drunk on raindrops, has the toot of his life. Wandering ascetics, unable to wander for a few months, gather on the high ground and talk about metaphysics, and, with them out of the way, it is the time for lovers. Eroticism, sensuality, and fertility are the dominant themes of the rainy season.

To a certain extent, of course, it depends on your vantage point. The conceit of the classical poet Kalidasa was that the rain clouds carried messages of love from a separated lover to his beloved. In the city today, people feel perhaps less sweet melancholy and more of other emotions, as they peer out through holes wiped in the fog on the windows of super-cooled offices or apartments, or wade through the thigh-deep water in a Calcutta street. Each monsoon, the story is heard of the pedestrian who has disappeared into the manhole that has had its cover removed to promote drainage, but I do not know the truth of it. I do have some knowledge of ankles wrenched because of stepping into potholes beneath the flood, and I often wonder, with acute discomfort, about rickshaw pullers, who do a lively business at this time of year and whose ankles are far more important to their meager living than mine are. There is good reason why, in the courtyard of the house in south Calcutta where I used to stay, miles from normal water, there is a still sturdy but now well-ventilated rowboat leaning against the wall. This boat is the *RB John H. Broomfield,* named after her owner, a jovial New Zealander and previous occupant, who saw not only little reason to get his nether parts wet but also the real possibility of being of service to invalids and others in the neighborhood whose lives were made particularly miserable by the annual excess of water. The *Broomfield,* like her owner, is full of years and noble service, but, unlike him, shows signs of it.

If you have occasion to fly over the plains, and especially the Ganges Delta region, during the rains, you will see hundreds upon hundreds of miles of water, with occasional villages sticking up through it, reflecting the lowering clouds, a dull, metallic gray. In one village an acquaintance of mine found it impossible, even after the water had receded, to consider moving back into his house, for while he had been away many snakes had moved in and found it to their liking. Some people seem to be able to treat these snakes like bothersome flies that keep getting into their beer, but I find I am more sensitive than that. "Haw," Lenny Walsh once said to me, "wait until you find a krait in your bath." I have always felt comfortable doing just as Lenny has instructed me, and the time I have spent waiting, I must say, has passed pleasantly and well.

These and similar matters were moving rapidly through my mind one time in the late summer of 1991, as my wife and I, in our house on Cape Cod, shrank trembling, as far away from the big front windows as we could get, during the hurricane that had for some reason been given the companionable name of "Bob." Though Bob was not on our calendar, thanks to modern technology we had had a couple of days' warning of his impending visit, and, unlike in some previous years, we had time to tape up the windows, fill the bathtubs with water, and lay in a supply of candles, lamp oil, and ice.

As we huddled at the back of the house, numbed by the all-pervasive sound, we could see, though barely, through the opaque, horizontal green wind, occasional vertical white streaks where there had been none before.

The realization that these were splitting trees was made the more shocking because none of the tearing and cracking and screaming could be heard above the roaring of the wind. My mind was so stunned by the noise and confusion that it was not until later that I realized that these were friends of fifty years that I was losing. Revelation 7:3 tells us that trees are friends and that we should not hurt them; God, of course, as CEO, can choose to ignore such interoffice memos, and does. The Bengali poet and novelist Rabindranath Tagore once likened the incomprehensible will of God to that of a small child who has laboriously built an elaborate castle of sand and then, impatient with the labor or its result, flattens it. Fifty years probably mean very little to God. I myself do not have fifty more and will not be around to see my sky filled with a different tracery. I am left, however, with the smaller and more finite joy of splitting the oak logs, and indeed, the occasional lucky stroke that cleaves the log with a satisfying thunk is compensation both great and petty.

After Bob had gone barging up the coast, slamming doors and kicking the cat in his mindless rage, my wife and I emerged from the house, completely shaken, to walk tentatively through the woods looking at the fallen pitch pines and the great Norway spruces that were big when I was a child, and, mostly, the oaks, usually not uprooted but broken off fifteen feet above the ground, as if someone with a huge scythe had gone through and mowed them all down. There must have been smaller tornadoes within the hurricane, for within a ribbon perhaps a hundred yards wide everything was flattened, and next to it was another ribbon in which two of every three trees still stood. We met our neighbors in the woods and talked with lowered voices, for that seemed appropriate. The silence, after the deafening roar of the storm, was complete, except for the dripping of water from the standing trees and the occasional crack of a weakened branch farther off in the woods.

In India, divine wrath is manifested not in the storm but in the absence of it. In the West, Mother Nature sighs at the adolescent antics of her children, perhaps smiles a little at the charm of their naive defiance, and waits until it is time to tuck them in and pull up the covers. Once in a while she quite understandably runs out of patience and delivers a quick backhander. In India she is less gentle and patient, perhaps because she has so much to do, but when she withholds her life-giving moisture, she is more than sending her children to bed without their supper. She is not often, thank God, that cruel.

In neither place do her children have the appropriate respect. But just as people tear the tops off the hills of Pennsylvania to get at the coal, so in India the timber merchants strip the Himalayan foothills in their greed. The rains tear the mountains loose from their footings and the water floods the defenseless plains in ways other than what was meant to be. God will, though in his own good time and not mine, put back my oaks and pines, and perhaps even the Himalayan and Pennsylvanian hills. If I were God I should like to do things my own way, though, without any help from loggers and developers. There is a story by a Bengali writer who goes by the pen name Bonaphul ("the forest flower"), in which he tells of the gods being increasingly burdened by the conflicting requests of humans seeking relief from the consequences of their own stupidity. The gods decide to take a nap until it all goes away.

PART III

*Rolling
Home*

Sober Men and True

*In which the author rolls toward home across the sea
and unexpectedly meets fierce warriors.*

If you have to leave India, by far the best way to do it is by British freighter from Calcutta. If it is 1958, there are only two or three of you as passengers, perhaps yourself and an Australian-Armenian merchant named Yahu Krustacian, a regular passenger twice a year on this ship between Calcutta and Cochin. The matter of customs is as pleasant as it can possibly be: the official comes aboard and has a quiet half-and-half with you as you sit under an awning on the deck and chats about manners and mores while friends drop by to see you off, and the ship bustles about getting ready for sea, the activity all the more satisfying because you have absolutely nothing to do with it, and he generally takes your word for it that things are as you say they are. You then get to sail for a long time down the Hughli River looking at the forms of aquatic life, which equal in

their variety and complexity their landbound counterparts, getting acquainted with your fellow passenger
and, later, those of immediate significance to you among
the ship's people. These of course include the captain,
who is really Robert Morley and who, with his officers,
will share his victuals with you over the next month or
so. The officers consist of a wide variety of mates, the
morbid but ubiquitous Scottish engineer named Mac-
Donald (there was an Admiralty Law entered, just after
the Restoration, that no British ship can put to sea without at least one MacDonald of the Isles; this law seems to
have been extended not only to the United States but
also into the twenty-first century, as *Star Trek* documents),
the ship's doctor, a cultured Londoner who has spent
his life trying to run away to sea and who looks at the
world as through the bottom of a glass, fuzzily, and, of
most significance, Yusuf the Barman, who is also dining
steward.

And there was just such a Yusuf on the *City of Blicester,*
the ship on which I left Calcutta in 1958 (my family having departed a couple of months earlier). Yusuf was a
slender, dignified, white-haired Lascar from Barisal in
Bangladesh (though in the days of which we speak, that
country had not yet found its identity), a place where
people go about in boats from the moment of birth. Las-
cars have manned British ships for centuries, and still do,
and Yusuf came from a long line of sailors. Unlike some

of the officers, he spoke English and a number of other
languages in addition to his native Bengali. He was smart
as hell and showed it by keeping his mouth for the most
part shut, whatever the provocation.

THE SHIP HAD SAILED in the afternoon, and it was
deep night before she moved out of the mouth of the
river and into the Bay of Bengal. As we moved offshore,
even if you had not been aware that the shore lights were
fading, you could not miss the beginnings of the ship's
roll and the change in her breathing as she moved into
the swells, a deep, slow whoooossssshhhaaah, a kind of
sigh of relief at getting away from the land at last and
into her own element, a long, reassuring breath that
meant that she was at ease and that her people could
be, too.

It also meant that the next morning the officers were
free to gather at the table, Yusuf serving. That first conversation, which probably was jovial, went something
like this:

> Krustacian: Aye sye, Third, fair dinkum myte this
> bloomin' fish's lookin' me royt in the oy; Yusuf, what
> kind o' tucker is this lad?
>
> Yusuf: . . . . (Wipes dessert plate.)
>
> Krustacian: What sye, Scotty? Too dingdong whacko
> you ask me cobber.

MacDonald: Aye, Yusuf, i' th' name o' th' wee mon, see th' oogliness o' 'oom starin' oop oot o' the plate balefully noo.

Yusuf: . . . . (Puts plate down.)

Robert Morley: Haw haw hmmmmph. Now gentlemen hmmmmph snort.

The passenger accommodations on the *City of Blicester* came very close to being gracious. There were three large cabins, all with private baths, writing desks, and comfortable chairs, and a very spacious common lounge, nicely appointed but used only when weather prevented one from being on the small sheltered deck just across the passageway aft, a step outside a sliding glass partition from the small bar at which Yusuf could be found at regulated but numerous hours of the day and night, ready to be of assistance to any passengers or off-duty officers who might have worked up a thirst. The doctor, with only two passengers and a rugged and healthy-looking crew to worry about, was quite often off duty and in a parched state pitiful to behold. Perhaps due to a hypermetabolic condition, his face was a permanent deep and glowing red, which, surrounded by his gray hair, made it look as if it was ready to broil a steak. For this, and for most conditions, his panacea was that seemingly accepted by most physicians in the East: a colleague of his, at dinner with us in Calcutta, had listened with a critical ear to the tearing cough that my wife and I were afraid would turn our infant son inside out and said, judiciously, "Peg o' rum'll fix him right up." It did, as a matter of fact. In any case, I would now and again bump into the doctor in the bar, the first time perhaps twenty minutes after the ship had slipped her cables. "No telling what creatures one might have picked up in Calcutta," he said. "Beastly place. Best to get them before they get you. Another whisky if you please, Yusuf."

The second mate was a thirsty blond person about my age, and it was either that fact or the bottle of Haig and Haig Pinch that I had brought aboard that drew us close at once. For although *Blicester*'s stores were seemingly endless, they were, unlike my Pinch, not without cost. I may flatter myself that it was more than the Haigian attraction that drew us together, but it is a fact that even after the Pinch had outlived its usefulness, a few hours into the voyage, we found ourselves together so much that I remember very little of Colombo, Cochin, or the Arabian Sea. I have, of course, snatches of memory: an afternoon in what must have been Ceylon, on the patio of a beautiful old hotel overlooking a white crescent-shaped beach bordered with green palms where, I was told later, a part of *The Bridge on the River Kwai* had been filmed; a city, I suspect Colombo, with broad streets and stuccoed buildings shining under a late-summer sun; and that same sun setting into the fading monsoon clouds with intense iridescent colors nearly impossible to imagine. And one impression is most vivid, that of sitting, for reasons I will touch upon, in the ship's lounge listening to the scores of *The Pajama Game* and *South Pacific,* with Ezio Pinza breaking my heart singing "This Nearly Was Mine."

The reason I was sitting in this lounge and not at the generous table with the others was that the Arabian Sea was, in August, just beginning to settle down after its annual monsoon frenzy; the breathing of *Blicester* was labored—less like her earlier deep sighs and more like someone who had been hit hard in the solar plexus— and I knew exactly how she felt. I had, therefore, sent word to Captain Morley that bangers and rashers of bacon were not high on my list of desiderata at that time, and that I therefore would not be joining him for breakfast that morning, or, quite possibly, ever again. My stomach had repositioned itself and was occupying the area just south of my larynx. The lounge was a place where a great deal of fresh air could be had, and it was far away from the galley, the mouth-watering aromas of which did not, just then, do their usual thing for me. And finally, as the second mate remarked when he courteously paid me a visit after breakfast, my greenish cast blended splendidly with the prevalent grays and mauves that dominated the decor of the place. The major disadvantage of the lounge was that it was in the superstruc-

ture of the ship and, being well above the center of grav-
ity, exaggerated the rolling and pitching quite a lot.

After what seems to me a decent interval of a day or
so, when *The Pajama Game* had so deeply impressed itself
upon me that to this day I cannot paddle a canoe across a
quiet inlet without hearing "Hernando's Hideaway," I
once again rejoined my hosts for a midday meal. The
captain, as I had foreseen, was as frisky as a St. Bernard
after the first snow and danced around inside his substantial frame, a sprightly if somewhat overweight elf.
"Haw," he said, "Haw, haw. Lamb stew for lunch, what?
Thought you Yanks were sailors, eh? Haw, haw, hmmmmph, snort."

"Extraordinarily salutary, seasickness," said the doctor
as the *City of Blicester* moved slowly into the ways of the
Port of Aden. "Purges the system." He carried his pint of
bitter from the bar to the little deck where I was sitting,
recovering my normal attractive shade of rose madder,
and remarking to my friend the second that I had been
unable, in India, to find the kind of sinuous hookah that
you normally see in illustrations of *The Arabian Nights*.
"Aden is just the place for you," he replied with certainty,
so when we had completed our anchorage and he had
finished his work, we set out in the least scruffy water-
taxi we could find, and, after a beer or two in a local
hotel (the second having observed that it would be an ab-
ject display of cowardice were I to give in to the noisy

and aerobic protests of my stomach), we set off for the hills. Aden is, at least in my memory, a dusty and scurfy kind of place, the Empire at that time being represented there by the usual marine, diplomatic, and mercantile appurtenances, but for the rest your average dismal sea-port town. The second scorned the few sorry curio shops along the waterfront and insisted that we go back into the hills behind, and so, in a hired battered yellow Austin, we did.

Some of the time that I had spent in India was dusty, and I was not unfamiliar with the grit hanging in the air even such a short time after that year's little rain had fallen, stirred up not only by our jaundiced passage but by that of camels and pleasant little overloaded donkeys and walking people. I was familiar with the way it had of getting into every available crevice. Familiar too was the gray-brown town of mud brick, baking in the oven of the surrounding mountains, to which the winding and dangerous track finally led. And sure enough, in the town square, a space big enough to turn the car around in, with the road entering on one side and low buildings on the other three, was the brass seller's shop. The second, in an English articulated, in deference to our Arabic-speaking environment, in his glottal area and with very great volume, instructed our driver to turn around and wait for us.

He did not have long to wait. The shop had been lifted

directly from *A Thousand Nights and a Night* and was daz-
zling in the afternoon sun, full of brasswork of the most
special and intricate decorations and wonderful shapes.
And there, on the front shelf, was exactly what I wanted
to buy in the way of hookahs. Five minutes after we had
arrived we had seen, bargained, and bought, and we
were leaving the shop for our taxi when it dawned on us
that the environment had changed dramatically. The village square, which had been completely devoid of people
when we arrived, was now full of warriors. It was as if,
while our backs had been turned, Cadmus had been by,
sowing the dragon's teeth. These were gaunt, bearded
specimens, too, carrying ancient but effective-looking
weapons, faces shadowed by the hoods of their bur-
nouses, clustered together in muttering groups that were
small but growing in number and rapidly filling the little
square. It occurred to me, of course, that these people
might be somewhat restless and irritable because the
British, in the very recent past, had acted testy about the
Suez Canal in particular and the disintegrating remains of
their Empire in general. I was also aware that my companion, in response to this hostility, was emitting tangi-
ble waves of electricity. It was clear that a little valorous
stupidity was in the offing, and I wanted no part of it. It
occurred to me that I might throw myself on the mercy
of the court, pleading that I was a poor colonial boy,
much like the court itself. I did not have to go that far,

fortunately for my self-respect, for it turned out that my companion's streak of decency was of quite the same dimensions as his streak of bravery, as is often true of the British character, and I was able to plead with some effectiveness the cause of my small children and their fatherless fate. We were both trembling—he with excitement at the proximity of battle and with indignation, I with terror—as we pushed our way through the crowd, which understandably grew still more restive when it was pushed, and got to our taxi. Our driver, a man of the world, needed no instructions, and we were off down the mountain before the doors had closed, all of us instinctively and absurdly hunching our shoulders against the fusillade that never, such was our good fortune, came.

Back on the ship, we passed through the Red Sea, the Mediterranean, and the Atlantic without further drama; *Blicester* arrived in Boston, eventually, and was greeted while still far at sea by the beautiful gaff-rigged schooner that brought our pilot to us. She rounded up with breathtaking grace on our leeward side, and the pilot swung aboard. It felt good to be home.

Barbarians Are at the Gates

◇◆◇

*In which the author is brought to grapple
with the nature of courtesy.*

Perhaps you don't know where you are in the scheme of things. Well, says the Rig-Veda, an ancient book of sometimes lengthy hymns, if you are not a Brahman, or a Warrior, or a People, or a Servant, or the sun or the moon or the wind, or a horse or some other animal with two rows of teeth, then you are, like me, an alien and a Barbarian. Some of the older Hindu texts also call us Yavanas or Greeks, or Mlecchas, whom the dictionaries define as those who don't speak Sanskrit, a substantial proportion of any given population, I would wager. In later times we were all called Ferengi, which is derived from the name Frank. It has always seemed to me a nearly incredible coincidence that all early European travelers to the subcontinent were named Frank, but it is one of the peculiarities of history, which has many. In Turkish, the name is pronounced with a Yiddish accent and signifies a European who has horses and a hat, and it is because of this that some scholars suggest that the origin of the word is Turkish. I myself have never owned any horses (I am afraid of them), and my hat was eaten by a camel in Port Said, but that is another story.

The Hindus are right in considering us barbarians, for whenever I come back from India the first thing I notice is the uncivilized way in which people behave. Children eat dinner with their baseball hats on backward. Courtesy has gone the way of the Palmer Method (which, for you latecomers, was not a means of birth control), the sidesaddle, the bunny hop, and the Marie Celeste, though they all, having once existed, are presumably still out there somewhere in space and time, perhaps in a parallel universe, sailing on some other seas. This is truly a great pity. As Judith Martin, or Miss Manners, has been trying to tell us for years, courtesy is far more than an outmoded, formal imposition of artificial behavior; it is, rather, the embodiment of cultural experience that guides us in how best to get on with one another, an evolved method of living together. It is certainly true that, as things get more and more crowded, it is increasingly difficult to avoid stepping on your neighbor's toes, but this merely suggests that the need for courtesy is now greater than ever before. It is not manifest. Getting along together does not seem to be a value just now.

It comes as something of a surprise to those who think of India as a crowded, ragged, and undernourished place to find that in fact India has learned over the years, as I have, that a degree of courtesy is both a moral and a practical imperative. Not too long ago when I was on an airport bus in India, a young man sprang from his seat as if it had sprouted thorns and said to me, "Sit here, *guruji,* please." (Although I am pretty spry for seventy, I appreciated it.) It used to be that way in the United States too, sometimes. And it is possible, of course, even in India, to find people who will push into lines in front of you and do other rude things; self-centeredness and lack of consideration for others may thus be a human rather than a cultural tendency. But I am always a little surprised to find it so prevalent in New England, a place that is associated in my mind with civility and little, rather than middle, fingers. I am afraid I must confess to having been deluded, for I find that there is in fact a long New England tradition of rudeness. If you had listened to the ascetic philosopher Henry David Thoreau while he was on Cape Cod writing a book about the place, you might have heard him remark that

A strict regard for truth obliges us to say that the few women whom we saw that day looked exceedingly pinched up. They had prominent chins and noses, having lost all their teeth, and a sharp W would represent their profile. They were not so well preserved as their husbands, or perchance they were well preserved as dried specimens. (Their husbands, however, were pickled.)

Now, while that might have been true (and may still be), it is not at all nice.

Manu might take exception to it, furthermore. He says that "a man should tell the truth and speak with kindness; he should not tell the truth unkindly nor utter lies out of kindness." New Englanders sometimes have the notion that the truth has to taste bad, like medicine, if it is going to do you any good. There is a kind of balance to the universe of your average Calvinist New Englander: my grandmother would look glumly out at a shimmering June day and say "We'll pay for it next winter."

In any case, it may well be that public transportation is the best way to keep your finger on the pulse, or in the United States the rap beat played at full volume, of the culture. I cannot but contrast the young man on the airport bus with the following exchange I heard in Chicago a while ago:

"Would you mind turning that radio down a little, please?"

"Why should I, fuh Chrissakes? It's mine, innit?" This came from a lad with a backward baseball cap who had placed his boom box down on the seat next to him and put his feet up on the seat opposite and was bouncing up and down and staring vacantly at the little old lady carrying a big package who was standing in front of him and trying vainly to reach the hanging strap.

Of course, this is not to say that daily social intercourse in India is all smiles and exultation. One would ordinarily think that when the daily grind becomes intolerable, the safest bet would be to go off and be a hermit. But even being a hermit does not necessarily help you control your temper. Look at circumstances surrounding the birth of the ascetic Durvasas ("Hard to Get Along With"): The story, and there is no reason to doubt it either, is that when Shiva and Brahma got into a fight, Shiva was so fierce in his anger that his wife Parvati said to him *Durvasam bhavati me,* or "Living with you has become a real problem." So Shiva, a real sweetie, got rid of his anger by placing it in the womb of a nice lady called Anusuya, who gave birth to Durvasas, and you can imagine what things were like after that.

But India seems to have more than its share of courtesy and culture. The epitome of it was the gentleman, a teacher at the Maulana Azad College of Calcutta University, scion of an old but now impoverished family, who would come every morning to try to teach me Persian. Even on the hottest days of May he would be wearing a full suit of fine but well-worn wool, with a high hooked collar in the Nehru fashion, and a long vest beautifully embroidered in blue and beige. He would look cool and composed as he recited to me as a daily greeting a long quotation from one of the classical Persian poets.

I guess we must still have that sort of thing in this country, too. I just haven't found it recently. There seems to be, rather, a burgeoning spirit of meanness. I don't know how to explain it. I have heard the theory of over-crowding, and how rats, when forced to rub shoulders constantly with one another, will grow short-tempered (how long-tempered they are to begin with is a matter for speculation). But India is far more crowded than the United States. Art Buchwald has attributed it to the drinking of coffee: he cites the case of the man who walked out of a coffeehouse and tried to knock down the Trump Building with his briefcase. (He didn't succeed, of course, but it was a good thought.)

In New York they have at least recognized the prob-lem, and I understand that the officials of the transit sys-tem thought it might help to redistribute passengers in the subway trains properly; crowds around the doors were hampering the efficient loading and unloading of passengers. So they painted large orange squares on the floor of the stations so that passengers entering the trains would know where the doors would be when the trains stopped and stay clear of those areas so that people could enter and exit the trains in an orderly way. I wonder if that worked.

Calcutta also has a subway, built over seemingly endless years by a combined Russian and Bengali team of engineers. There were many weisenheimers among us who made jocular predictions, before it opened, about how it would be the world's longest urinal, and how trying to keep it pumped out, since the highest point in Calcutta is six feet above sea level, would blow the electrical grid sky-high. Well, according to every report (I have not yet ridden on it), the subway is clean, dry, smells like a rose, has stations with mosaics of paintings by Rabindranath Tagore, is fast, and is peopled by citizens who keep the stations spotless and who do not push and shove.

We Franks, perhaps, could learn to be less hasty in our judgments.

Aliens Among Us

*In which the author realizes that things are
not always what they seem.*

There are in this world some alien things
that seem familiar and yet change their
shapes before your very eyes. I call to
mind one bright, clear day in Pune, when I had left the
gate to the little garden of my bungalow standing open,
and a passing water buffalo had wandered in to eat my
marigolds, which were sparse but tempting. It is hard to
know how to introduce water buffaloes to you, if you do
not know any; maybe the best way is to say that inside a
body the size of a well-grown hippopotamus with long
curly horns there dwell at least two creatures. One is a
placid, somewhat stupid, marigold-eating dolt. The other,
recognized by much Indian mythology, which knows
about these things, is a bloody-eyed, densely packed, two-
ton container of unmitigated fury (I once ran into one
when I was on a bicycle, and I can tell you firsthand that

it is a very solid creature). Being at that time new to buffaloes, I saw at first only the easygoing domestic cow of
my youth, though on a somewhat grander scale, and I
therefore threw a rock at it to indicate my proprietary
feeling for my marigolds. The cow was instantly replaced
by a raging, malevolent thing—the bad person struggling to get out had been released—as I, in turn, was
transformed from a spindly provider of marigolds to a
hostile alien form that threw stinging things and was,
therefore, to be eliminated at once in order to restore
equilibrium to the environment.

The buffalo missed me, though not by much, and
went headfirst into the post supporting the veranda roof.
I drove by the bungalow not too long ago, thirty years
after the event, and the post and roof are still arranged in
an interesting V-shape.

Other things change more slowly. When we came
back to this country, one of the first things that we noticed was that the crustacean loosely called "the lobster"
had gained immensely in popularity. In India they have
what they call lobsters in English, but which in reality are
bara chingri, "humongous prawns," which swim around in
the water and eat other prawns and are so popular in the
western part of Bengal that they have become the symbol, perhaps even the totem, of the local football team
(their major rivals, the East Bengal club, are the Hilsa
Fish). When I was very young, lobsters were considered

good for little except fertilizer (as our Indian friend Squanto had pointed out to the Pilgrims, who were curious about how to plant things). They were certainly not the rarefied delicacies that they have become today. Perhaps things will change again when word of their true nature and taste in luncheon gets out: they eat whatever they find at the bottom of Boston Harbor, and the lobster fishermen are complaining about the recent cleanup of that unhealthy place, saying that their lobsters will not live there anymore.

My brother told me about a friend of his who decided that, the price of lobsters being what it was and rising, he should go into the lobster-raising business and get in on the action. So he bought a few acres of mudflat in Maine (this was years ago, before they had put condominiums on it all), fenced it off so that his lobsters could not wander away to sea at high tide, threw some small crustaceans into the tidal pools, and went away. When he came back, what he had was one vast female lobster, for it is well known that in this corner of nature, females are more voracious, ferocious, contumacious, and also bigger than their male counterparts.

So there are some parallels that can be drawn between the homarid situation and the hominid one, and also some distinctions that can be made. One of the distinctions is that lobsters seem to be on the whole fairly forthright in the expression of their exclusiveness: when a lobster says "I vant to be alone," it means it. This may be because lobsters do not have consciences. I must speculate here, of course, but it seems unlikely that lobsters find it necessary to isolate others psychologically and linguistically before eating them, the way boys, another example of a primitive life form, seem to do, as William Golding has pointed out so well.

It is not uncommon to consider as "Other" that which does not fit readily into preconceived packages and personal understanding (it is perhaps less common to recognize that using such preconceptions in the initial stages of an acquaintanceship is necessary). I observe that Minister Farrakhan distances white or pink-skinned people from the human race by teaching that these people were created not by God, who is good and therefore incapable of such offensive behavior, but by an evil person called Yacub, who in fact spilled something during a lab experiment and unleashed the white race on the earth like a plague of locusts (etymologically related to the word *lobster,* by the way); it is very like the killer bee phenomenon of more recent days. This of course is in reponse to a long, tedious, and far less colorful list of ways in which the pinks have sought to put blacks in some category other than "human," so that they would be justified in what would otherwise be unacceptable speech, attitude, and behavior. Nor is it possible to escape completely one feminist theory that seeks to accomplish the same in a very creative way: the ultimate source of patriarchy is UFOs. The ultimate Otherness is completely alien.

If I understand it correctly, there are two subsets to the theory. The first one holds that the aliens from these UFOs found some nice men standing around and persuaded them without too much difficulty that what they needed was power; this is also the milder aspect of the theory, for it allows the possibility that while men have always been gullible and, perhaps, lazy, they have not always been stinkers: there is nothing genetically too far wrong, and education and a firm hand will eventually bring things back to an equilibrium. The other interpretation is more radical, for it holds that the aliens from the UFOs are themselves the patriarchs. This, apart from parthenogenesis, holds out little hope for the human race, and is stunningly pessimistic. I must say that when I first read this interpretation, like Hortensio in *The Taming of the Shrew* when he was hit on the head by Katherina, "I stood amazèd for a while, as on a pillory, looking through the lute."

More acceptable to me is the idea of patriarchs as warlike folk—a picture of Genghis Khan pops to mind —"from the barren fringes of the globe," "leaving destruction and devastation in their wake." That is more like the patriarchs I know, and this interpretation is given credence by books with titles like *Leadership Secrets of Attila the Hun,* by Wess Roberts, Ph.D., that spring at you from mail-order catalogs. And this, of course, brings us back to the question of lobsters, for it is possible to notice that one of the characteristics of international cartels is a kind of lobster mentality: the lobster, unable or unwilling to make subtle distinctions in its tiny brain, gobbles up its neighbors because everything is itself anyway, because that is the way lobsters do things, and because the neighbors are there, and shouldn't be.

Specifying the genesis and identification of evil, and placing responsibility for it squarely on the shoulders of someone else, gets pretty earthy. In the *Janganama,* a text by an eighteenth-century Bengali Muslim writer named Hayat Mahmud, there is a story that evil came about through Yazid, who was the murderer of the grandsons of the Prophet. Yazid was not himself entirely responsible, however, for one night his father had been squatting to relieve himself when he was stung on the lingam by a scorpion. "Never in my life," he said, later recollecting the experience in tranquillity, "have I known such pain." God, being empathetic, wanted to send some medicine, but the angel (some angel!) Jibrail dissuaded him from doing so, arguing that God should not disrupt the flow of history. Not only does this story remind us that we don't know what pain is (it is nowadays called "discomfort"), but it places the generation of evil on the poison-polluted appendages of Yazid's father, providing feminists with ammunition they do not really need. It also allows

everyone to place ultimate responsibility on the scorpion, which nobody much likes anyway, and which, I
need not remind you, looks like a miniature lobster with
a double-jointed tail.

There is a sixteenth-century Bengali text called the
Chandimangala, in which the protagonist, a merchant, is
lost at sea in a fog. There is nothing like being lost at sea
in a fog to put things into their proper perspective, to
tell you where you are, or perhaps where you are not, to
bring about an awareness of the tenuousness of everything in the terror of a separation from all that is familiar
or friendly to people. The blatting of foghorns and the
screaming of the whistles of huge invisible vessels that
could be ten miles or ten yards away is disorienting;
forests of masts appear and disappear in the fog (to our
merchant, they are the feelers of immense prawns), and
a huge reef heaves up out of the water just on your leeward side, dark and ugly and covered with barnacles, so
close that you can hear the sucking sound, with twelve
feet hanging down and six heads, and you do not look
upon this gladly; and then, by some miracle, or perhaps
because you have not eaten the kine of Helios, you are in
the calm water behind the rocks.

Things did not stop with the prawn antennae, for our
agitated merchant, either, for there in the middle of the
ocean he comes across a beautiful woman sitting on a
lotus. The poet, leaving the merchant to his astonish-

ment, dwells for a while, with much affection, on the details of her rounded form, the ten moons floating at the ends of her fingers and toes, and her reddened hands, which put to shame the redness of the lotus on which she sits. But then even the poet's mind is boggled, for the lady is eating and regurgitating elephants and, once in a while, she gets to her feet and does a little dance.

That, now, is alien, and the poet agrees. "I cannot understand the actions of that young woman," he says. But then again, despite the elephants and the sober expression on her face, she may be dancing just to express her simple pleasure at meeting somebody way out there in the middle of nowhere. I know I would be. Things aren't always what they seem, you know.

Beau Geste

In which the author is taught about grunts and gestures in modern American English.

It is no news to anybody that language is more than words. We all have not only palates, glottises, tongues, and so on, but other parts of the body as well: gestures of the head, hands, and buttocks, for example, are quite as laden with significance as are words. They are like words in the sense that they form a bridge between the self and the rest of humanity; like spoken language, they have the unique power to bring into existence that which was not there before.

Some gestures cross cultural boundaries, and others are culturally fixed. Pointing at an object, for instance, is a gesture commonly understood, though it may differ from culture to culture in its level of perceived courtesy (how many times did you hear your mother say, "Don't point, it's not polite"?). But pointing is also a gesture that, despite being primary, is not without subtlety and ambiguity. Let me cite an example.

Soon after getting back from India I was driving my van along a street where both curb lanes were filled with parked automobiles. I had slowed down a great deal in order to allow a car coming from the other direction to pull into my lane and get around a delivery truck temporarily parked in the driving lane. The driver of the car behind me, extremely anxious, as it turned out, to pick up his girlfriend one hundred yards down the street, pulled out and accelerated past me, causing both me and the driver of the car coming in the opposite direction to slam on our brakes to avoid colliding with him. My English, of course, failed me, and my heart nearly did also. My Japanese van, however, was made of sterner stuff, and emitted that high-pitched bleat that Japanese cars emit when stressed. The offended driver who had just passed me glared into his rearview mirror, rolled back his sunroof, and pointed urgently upward several times with his middle finger. And there in the sky was a seagull tracing lazy circles, which I would have missed had it not been for the language common to me and my fellow driver, though my mother would have called his pointing impolite.

Despite the fact that such gestures are of a primary level of signification, and perhaps logical extensions of the emotional states that are associated with them, there are, as I suggested, many possibilities of ambiguity. I once saw the gesture just described used by Larry Bowa when he played for the Chicago Cubs. Larry had hit a triple over the heads of the drawn-in outfield, clearing the bases and winning the game, and the TV camera focused on him as he was waving this same greeting to a fan who had evidently been heckling him. The gesture must have seemed arcane to a number of others besides me, for Steve Stone felt obliged to interpret it to the vast television audience: "He's saying 'We're number one,' Harry."

If interpretations of these gestures are necessary within our own culture, it would be reasonable to assume that their additional nuances and complexities across cultural boundaries require even more explanation. In addition, across these boundaries they not infrequently become tangled up with a whole other set of gestures indigenous to the other culture. While it is not absolutely necessary to learn the beautiful language of the hands—the mudras or gestures of some of the dances of India—in order to learn the Hindi or the Tamil language, the graceful *namaste* gesture or greeting, in which one puts one's palms together and raises them to the forehead, or one of the variations of the Muslim salutation, in which one raises one's cupped hand to one's forehead, is indispensable. But I would caution the reader to remember the case of the Indian student who, after a year spent in association with young Americans, grew to assume that the middle-fingered gesture so popular with these Americans was in fact a shorthand or slang form of the *namaste,* and so used it for a time before the impediment was corrected.

Kinesthetics aside, when learning another language one must become sufficiently acculturated to the environment in which that language is spoken to be able to interpret it properly. One hears what one expects to hear. When General Colin Powell was visiting Prime Minister Yitzhak Shamir some years ago, he greeted the prime minister in Yiddish, which he had learned as a boy. The prime minister stared at him for a long minute, until the general asked "Don't you understand?"

So gestures are not the only possible means of communication. You can also speak in words, and scholars have spent their lives considering the implications of this. The human mind's compulsion to impose order upon its environment, warranted or not, its penchant for shaping sound into paradigmatic patterns and making those patterns differ from place to place across the globe, have kept many linguists productively occupied over the centuries. In India, which is a place where they have a good deal to say about most things—language coming in for its share—there is a feeling that one is bound to respect, a feeling that of all possible language only three-quarters is overt, the rest being hidden and ready to burst forth at any time. It is perhaps this that causes many of our finest minds to dig ghoulishly around in linguistic cemeteries (in India, Sanskrit may not be dead but merely comatose, for, if my memory serves, in the last census 329 people claimed to be speakers of that language). Or perhaps it is the comfort provided the solitude-seeking scholar by these languages. It is nice and quiet in there. No one talks to you, and there is no necessity to try to talk to them. Communication in such situations is reflexive, much as in prayer, and it would be more upsetting than anything else if one were to get an immediate and verbal response. These scholars will be very surprised when, one day when they are digging away, their shovels sink in up to the haft and the fourth part of language comes whooshing out like an overcrowded cocktail party and bites them on the ankle.

And this is not the only surprising thing that may take place. Among the most curious lines in all of English literature is in the preface to William Dwight Whitney's *Sanskrit Grammar* (my friend Gerry Kelley used to say that, as is true in this case, prefaces are often far more entertaining than the books they preface):

It was in June, 1875, as I chanced to be for a day or two in Leipzig, that I was unexpectedly invited to prepare the Sanskrit grammar for the Indo-European series projected by the Messrs. Breitkopf and Hartel.

The casualness with which this remark is offered makes one wonder whether Whitney was in fact surprised at all; there is a certain debonair quality to it, a suaveness. A lot of nineteenth-century scholars were like that, assuming the world to be their pork chop, but Whitney was clearly the Fred Astaire of the community:

"Ah, Whitney. Nice to see you for a day or two here in Leipzig. As long as you're here, would you mind preparing us a Sanskrit grammar?"

"Why [flicking a bit of lint off his sleeve], not at all. When did you say you might need it? [Tappety tap tap, TAP TAP!]"

But perhaps Whitney just happened to be at the right place at the right time. The nineteenth century swarmed with scholarly, and especially linguistic, swashbucklers. Richard Burton (of *Arabian Nights,* not Elizabeth Taylor, fame) of course comes immediately to mind, and brave, eerie, diamond-eyed fellows like Charles ("Chinese") Gordon. G. W. Joy's painting, which appears on the cover of John H. Waller's biography of the extraordinary Gordon, sums it up: Gordon seems to be looking at his wristwatch as if to check the time, while he is about to be impaled on the spearpoint of a Sudanese Anwar person.

A less-well-known case is that of John Beames, who was collector and commissioner of the Bengal presidency from 1861 to 1893 and some kind of philologist, let me tell you. Beames chested a swathe through academia with little of the oversensitive pussyfooting, or scientific objectivity, so typical of scholars today. He by no means limited his remarks to the linguistic and other affairs of the Indian subcontinent. He wrote that he found in all places and climes "pedants and grumblers," the "Saxon clods of the time of the Conqueror," for example, "who objected to the terms beef, veal, pork, and mutton, which were supplanting his pure English ox, calf, pig, and sheep." (The Normans can be accused of many things, but brevity of memory is not among them.) I am rather thankful for this, for I cannot really hear myself ordering calf scallopini at Seraglio's Italian Villa.

Beames didn't care for Germans at all, nor for their language, of which he said that "its usefulness as a practical, working, everyday speech is far below that of English or any other European language," as it consists of "the unpleasantly harsh collision of consonants." In the nineteenth century that was considered politically okay, in fact, rather dashing.

U.S. Power Squadron

*In which the author is forced to reflect on the gender
of boats and on parallel universes.*

The word for "power" in the Sanskritic languages is *shakti,* and, interestingly, a general name for the Goddess is also Shakti: she is the force that energizes the rest of the universe, and in the iconography she is seen dancing on the chest of a male deity who is dead, or at least sleeping, or watching football. The term *empower* does not seem to mean, as it is coming to increasingly in this country, to gain control of a universe that is ever expanding outward from wherever you may be standing. The fact is that power blurs fine distinctions, as Dr. Frankenstein discovered, and stimulates the perception of a world that contains the same forms that everyone else sees, but gives these forms different meanings. It stimulates what Plato and John Everett III, in different contexts, call parallel universes.

I remember this idle thought wandering through my mind some years ago as I gazed, with some envy, at a television screen on which then-president Bush was dashing among the rocks and reefs of what looked for all the world like coastal Maine in his big blue power boat *Fidelity*. *Fidelity* is not a good name for this boat. A big blue power boat should have a name like *Avenger* or *In-yourface* or *Neptune's Belch* or, in the mode of the day, *Domination*. *Fidelity* is a soft, considerate, inspiring name, feminine, if I may say so, and conveying little of the snarling, bullying, petulant aggressiveness more typical of big blue power boats and of the degendered guardians of the seraglio than of its graceful inhabitants. Big blue power boats have very little to do with gender, in fact, just as muscle cars have little to do with transportation, or power lunches with nourishment.

But it is a democratic age, and the hostile statement made by such power boats has been brought within every wastrel's price range in the form of something called the jet ski, which is a concentrated form of irritating, self-important uselessness. This jet ski has become so familiar a part of our deteriorating environment that it has even been given an acronym: it is called a PWC (pronounced "pwick"), standing for "Personal Water Craft." A boating magazine to which I no longer subscribe recently spent a lot of valuable space trying to convince me that a pwick is actually a boat, and that the operators of these aquatic

abominations are mariners and thus due the respect ac-
corded members of that calling, and that I should not be
such a dinosaur about evolutionary change above the surface tension. The magazine did not succeed, in part because the next several pages were filled with ads from
Yamaha and Kawasaki, who manufacture these things,
but it did bring about a noticeable change in tension
below the surface, which provided me with a ruddy,
hale-fellow-well-met look and brought me compliments
on my health. A PWC, I continue to hold, is to a boat as
a gnat is to a lark: they share a medium in which to
move, and that is about it. The power of the jet ski, I
might finally observe, lies not in bluster and brutality, as
is the case with its larger relative the big runabout-type
power boat, but in its whining voice. In both cases the effect is the same, that of calling attention to itself. PWCs,
ridden by people mesmerized by the sensation of speed
and simulated danger, which pass within feet and very
real danger of my swimming grandchildren, certainly do
draw my attention.

I must hasten to say that it is not my belief that engines
have somehow turned on their creators and become the
enemies of mankind, the way the computer Hal did. *Enemies* is perhaps too strong a word. I would rather say that
engines have simply strayed from the purpose for which
they were intended. Their purpose was, like that of
speech and laughter, to distinguish people from other ac-

cidents of nature (or, if you are religious, Divine Mistakes). But somewhere along the line there seems to have been a miscalculation, and once such has been made, waves of disaster follow, spreading out through history like the wake behind a garbage scow. I am not, in other words, talking about my cousin the Nantucket scalloper who goes quietly about making his living in his watch cap and sweatshirt, his boat caulked with roofing tar and badly needing its annual coat of house paint from Sears. There is in his world no screaming for attention. The difference between the chugging of this fisherman as he leaves the harbor early in the morning mist and the whine of a pwick or a high-powered outboard is a significant one.

My brother, George, and I used to have a tiny schooner named *Isis;* in that schooner there was an immense engine, which would crouch in its great mahogany box, taking up most of the space in the cockpit, smirking self-absorbedly, entirely indifferent to the discomfort of those who were merely trying to coexist with it. To its credit, it must be said that you could never actually catch it smirking. When you lifted the top of its box it would be sitting there with its eyes closed, playing possum. It was not until we got to know it quite well that we began to realize that in fact it could barely contain its chortles, for it knew its intentions, and we did not. My brother frequently claimed that this engine hated us (sometimes allowing, with adjectives and gerunds, that for him the feeling was mutual). I would rather consider that it was merely being indifferent to our welfare. Like any larger and older sibling it would tease and play too rough, rarely satisfied until its younger sibling broke into tears. I did this fairly often, and then, sometimes at least, the engine would relent and begin to chuckle and pop in its deep, soothing voice and agree to take us for a ride to the end of the channel. Usually, feeling that it had done enough for the day, or because of simple mischief or testiness, it would stop there and leave us on our own.

It is my feeling that it is very difficult to get people to understand these problems. One calm and sweltering day, when we were fitting Isis out and trying to get the engine to turn over, a young dock attendant remarked, "Columbus didn't need a motor, why should you?" My brother good-naturedly offered him a greasy wrench in reply, which he ducked.

One reason why Columbus didn't need an engine is that he didn't have to go two miles up a narrow, twisting channel against the wind to make his mooring. For indeed, that was the situation of the anchorage in which *Isis* lived. The channel opened to the southwest, included two ninety-degree turns, and was in some places no more than thirty feet wide. This made getting out into the open water on the prevailing southwest wind a problem that we needed the engine's cooperation to solve, though getting in was a cinch, if one's nerves were strong enough to take the necessary jibes and one was nimble enough to avoid the shift lever and control handles the engine was forever trying to trip one with.

Isis's hull, then fifty years old (she had worked hard as a fishing boat and was now retired to a life of relative luxury), built in Nova Scotia of hackmatack, was reliable and full of old-world values and thus usually not a co-conspirator in the games the engine played. Once in a while the mechanical and electrical accessories would persuade her that it might be fun to spring a small leak and run the batteries down with pumping, but it did not come naturally to her. This sort of thing so convulsed the engine, though, that when asked it would be able to do no more than cough for a minute before subsiding into its usual ill-natured silence. I could not in good conscience claim that *Isis* was completely devoid of a sense of mischief. Occasionally, despite her age and dignified bearing, she would take more pleasure than was seemly in sweeping her nine or so tons and her antsy crew down the narrow channel, having tricked us into setting all her sails in a twenty-five-knot breeze on her quarter, through the middle of a fleet of thirty-five small racing boats with blue sails, her skirts spreading gracefully in her train. But this was rare, and by and large she was exemplary in her dignity and forebearance.

On a day that comes to mind, we were moving down

the channel toward the anchorage, the wind on the quarter, the engine having quit, as usual, the tide at rest. It
was extraordinarily pleasant and quiet. The wind was
easy, the outgoing traffic was light, my brother and I
were relaxed, the schooner was making contented bur-
bling noises as she made her way in miniature majesty toward her mooring. My brother, rejoicing that we did not
have to be concerned, as we so often did at this stage of
the voyage, about the spar-cracking jibe sometimes necessary in the tiny basin crammed with jewel-encrusted
yachts that we had to navigate to make our mooring, had
already popped the top off the first of his cans of beer.
We were well to our side of the channel, just on the line
between light- and dark-colored bottom, in the bottle-
neck where the channel is narrowest—a delicate time
even under these, the best of circumstances—when my
brother, who was sitting with his back against the cabin
trunk, gazing over the stern into the middle distance
with a placid, not to say vacant, look on his face, suddenly began to turn red. It was just as if someone had
been painting him, from the neck slowly upward, with a
spray can of alizarin crimson. I of course inquired as to
his health, and in response he choked and pointed to the
channel mouth whence we had come. The huge signs
placed at short intervals all along the channel, saying in
ten-foot letters such things as NO WASH SIX MPH SLOW
NO WAKE CAUTION, might as well have been written in

Twi, if indeed Twi is written, for all they registered with the oblivious gentleman at the wheel of a sixty-foot monster coming toward us at close to the speed of sound, throwing a gigantic wash, the roaring of her engines drowning out that of the small-boatmen plunging in her wake (which was described by one despairing cry heard above the crashing of the waves as "that huge thing you're dragging behind you"). Just as the monster drew abeam of us, the red color reached the roots of my brother's hair and smoke began to issue, at first only in slight whisps, from his ears. Previous to this, I had thought that the Sanskrit poets were merely using hyperbole when they described an angry person's eyes as revolving in his head; my brother's eyes were in fact spinning like pinwheels. Under most circumstances the mildest of men—if I had a criticism it would be of his occasional tendency to jettison wrenches and provisions prematurely—he hurled the can, though it was still half full, against the glistening flank of the leviathan, which was then about ten feet away.

I do not always think good things about boats made of plastic. This, however, I shall have to confess: when struck with authority by half-full beverage cans, they resound like bass drums, very satisfactorily. The boat's driver (I cannot bring myself to call him anything else), his eyes bulging out and his gold-braided cap flying off his head just like in a Warner Brothers cartoon, slammed the boat into reverse. She, her engines grinding and screaming unrepeatable oaths, came to a reluctant stop. The driver, less concerned, I am sure, about the canoe with the three children in it that he might have run down than with the dent in his hull, rushed to the bow of his boat, which was pitching madly in its own wake, to ascertain how big a dent a canoe can make. I would like to think that it was a newfound concern for his fellow mariners that caused him to continue his journey at a more reasonable pace. Whatever the reason, he did so, ignoring those boatmen who were still bobbing about in the channel waving their fists and shouting salty imprecations, and my brother and me, who were, wholly unnecessarily, as it turned out, whistling and studying the cloud formations for signs of a waterspout.

Apart from what Freud has to say on the matter of boats and symbols, certain kinds of boats, like certain kinds of cars, symbolize only desire for power over your environment. As I mentioned, this desire for power is androgynous. If you would not mind switching back to the previous channel for a minute, you would find that a gentle northerly is blowing, for as Ecclesiastes says, "The wind goeth toward the south, and turneth about into the north, it whirleth about continually," and that's a fact. You would also find *Isis* making her modest way seaward, wing and wing, evoking those looks of admiration that constitute the point of being an old wooden boat. She was perhaps halfway down the channel when ahead of us appeared an immense vessel, far too big, it seemed, for that little strip of water, and getting bigger by the second. There was a psychedelic moment in which I was convinced that some intersection of worlds had taken place in which *Isis* was about to go head-on into the *QE II.* We got as far as we could to the right side of the channel, jibed the mainsail and staysail so that we were no longer wing and wing, and the monster, moving in silence except for the swoosh of her hull, so soft that we could hear the tinkle of glasses and cocktail conversation from the deck high above us, was by. Our keel brushed the sand, but no damage was done, and as we looked up, in mild shock, at her retreating transom, it was difficult to avoid noticing her name: *Elizabeth R.* I remembered reading that one Ms. Taylor, an actress, I believe, in a flicker called *National Velvet,* was in town for a horse show. Looking back on it, I find it possible to be impressed by the modesty of the statement, for there was plenty of room to have added *Dei Gratia Regina*—or maybe that was Victoria.

In conclusion, it is nice to have power, when you are caught in the tidal rip off Woods Hole, or when you are two runs down in the ninth. When I was growing up, the Red Sox had a series of barrel-chested, four-lettered persons playing first base, all of whom could hit the ball very great distances with reasonable frequency. There was always, for some reason, more admiration for this power than for the controlled grace of Williams's swing. Or maybe I'm just getting crotchety. I hear the sound of triangular metal spikes clicking down the long, dark concrete corridor, suddenly silent out on the grass. It sounds like distant, slightly out-of-synch trains clicking slowly over rail joints. Or maybe it's only acorns dropping onto the veranda deck. They fall earlier every year, it seems.

Ludi, Ludi

In which the author discovers a strange language,
spoken by white-clothed cultists.

The Brits and I both left things behind us in India. I left a substantial piece of myself. The Brits left a wide variety of things more lasting: railroads and such appendages of them as the peculiar brick Gothic architecture found in the Victoria Railway Terminus in Bombay, a legal code to stack on top of the two or three already in place, teatime, and an odd language most often heard spoken by groups of lunatics dressed in white clothes and floppy hats, most of whom stand idly around on plots of open space while two of their number run back and forth between bunches of sticks tied together. The exchange is emulated by cricket writers in the otherwise English-language newspapers:

In not a moment over six or eight hours' play, the score went from 240 to 780, and it was at that very moment that the fun started. Paramashivam, in for Ranade, who was in for Abdullah, had taken two wickets on two successive balls, and his third was a snorter that skidded by the batter Rahim ankle-high and swoggled his stumps. "Played, well played, by Jove," was the cry from the crowd at the first game of the Test, who applauded wildly as Rahim removed his hat and presented it to Paramashivam. Chatterji was out leg before after, and in frustration Shivaji Singh lifted Paramashivam and carried him to mid-off, where he was nicely taken by Surendrenath Sen. It was at this point that drinks arrived.

None too soon, either, if you ask me.

Some of this nearly incomprehensible language has made its way into more normal English. My wife gave me for my last birthday (well, I certainly hope it does not turn out that way) a book by Robert Hendrickson called *Salty Words*. It is not only full of such information as what you call a group of turtles (a bale of turtles) or of jellyfish (a smack of jellyfish) but also explains that the nautical expression "shiver me timbers" is not nautical at all, but refers to the attitude assumed by the wooden wickets when struck by the cricket ball. I will tell you a story that may or may not shed some light on this controversy.

Once upon a time there was, in now-familiar waters, a beautiful old ketch. She had been built all of teak in Thailand about the turn of the century but was found abandoned and rotting in a corner of a boatyard on Martha's Vineyard. She was lovingly restored to her original uncommon beauty by the tender ministrations of a salt-encrusted old gentleman from Rhode Island. Her name was *Shalimar,* after that loveliest of gardens in Kashmir conceived by the Mughal emperor Jahangir and completed by Shah Jehan (both loved Kashmir, though Jahangir found the wine a little sour). *Shalimar* the boat was about forty-five feet long and gaff-rigged on both masts, and with her salt-whitened decks of narrow teak planks curving to her elegant shape, she was a sight worth seeing. Worth seeing also was the way her skilled skipper wheeled her about the harbor.

One evening, I was enjoying a sundowner on the deck of the boat owned by my friends Jim and Ginny, watching the stunning old ketch come rolling down the channel, all sails set and glowing gold as butter in the late summer evening sun.

"Gorgeous, inshe, Ginny?" I said.

"Betcher bird," said Ginny.

Jim, however, was watching with a more critical eye.

"'Pears to me," he said, "like skipper's got a drop too much of the creature aboard of um, aye."

He squinted thoughtfully as the ketch swung her nose gracefully into the wind, came up well short, and ran up on the afterdeck of the sixty-foot gold-plated sloop moored at the neighboring berth. This sloop was the talk

of the harbor, not only because of her immaculate main-
tenance but because no one had ever seen her leave the
dock. The only thing that proved she was not painted
there was the ever-changing slew of beautiful women always draped around her decks and rigging. She was
owned by a tired-looking man in a braid-decorated cap,
and it was onto her deck that *Shalimar* rose majestically,
her twelve-foot bowsprit thrusting slowly into the sloop's
rigging like the saber of Lord Cardigan leading the
charge at Balaklava, scattering damsels left and right.
When the grinding and cracking and screaming had
stopped, a mutter broke the stunned silence. "Shivered
her timbers good, by Jaysus," said Jim. At least, that's
what I think he said. It's what I would have said, anyway,
if I could have said anything.

But even apart from India's acceptance of the strange
language of cricket, there must have been some intrinsic
appeal to the game itself. As my friend Ramanujan used
to say, a culture does not accept from another that which
is not already latent in itself. There must have been
something very like cricket (and football, too) seething
just below the surface of the culture of South Asia, waiting, like language, to burst forth. In Calcutta, and for
that matter everywhere in South Asia, every reasonably
level spot that does not have a building or a somnolent
cow resting on it is a cricket pitch. In Calcutta, the
maidan, the vast, open grassy area in the west-central

part of the city, is covered at all times by groups of boys and young men playing one or another of these games, or field hockey (if you really think that field hockey is always played by high-school girls in tartan skirts, I'm going to put you in goal with two enormous, hairy Sikhs on a breakaway, beards flying, charging down on you, passing that hard little ball back and forth between them, and let you wonder which one is going to make the shot that removes your head). And on the day of a major football match between, let us say, the East Bengal and the Mohanbagan football clubs, Calcutta is a madhouse. The World Series ain't in it, as Patrick O'Brian might say.

Football is of two basic varieties. One is rugby football, a rough blocking and tackling game similar to ours, and the other is soccer. Both inspire high emotion and, as is true elsewhere in the world, sometimes lethal enthusiasm, and fans have been known to smuggle knives and bottles into some of the more intense matches, with which to express the profundity of their loyalties.

Both forms of the sport have an illustrious history in Calcutta, dating at least from 1854, when a game was played between the Calcutta Club of Civilians and the Gentlemen of Barrackpore; the next colossal struggle was between The Etonians and The Rest, in 1868, won by Eton, three to zip. These games were intra-British rivalries (not the less vigorous for that, as the merchants, or *jutewallas,* as they were called, were scorned by both the military and the civil administrators, who disliked one another, too, and feelings were returned in kind, doubled). But Bengalis, attracted by the noise and heat, soon got involved, and the Mohanbagan Club, made up entirely of Bengalis, was founded in 1878. It soon became a nationalist symbol, and games against the Brits became miniature struggles for independence; a well-placed elbow or a surreptitious kick in the groin were giving a little of its own back to the Raj.

Those Brits who could see over the rims of their teacups could discern the day when there would in fact be no more Raj. The next best thing, they figured, would be to have an educated elite, English in everything but complexion, in place to run things, and various schools and universities, and attitudes of one sort or another. Football and cricket were indispensable parts of this social engineering. India, of course, accepted the parts of this that it wanted to, tucked those away in nooks and crannies of its own literature and culture, and went on its way, as it generally does, humming a song by Rabindranath Tagore.

The Brits perhaps did not realize at the time, as they have come to today, surveying the wreckage that follows a soccer match in Birmingham or Copenhagen, that sports teams inspire a pugnacious loyalty equaled only sometimes by jingoistic patriotism. Or maybe they did. In any case, divisions already existing in the society were exacerbated, for the Mohammedan Sporting Club was founded soon after the largely Hindu Mohanbagan, and the international Brits vs. Indians rivalry took on an added, even more heated, internecine dimension.

It did not, and does not now, matter that not all members of Mohammedan Sporting are Muslims (the club in fact introduced to India the curious concept of the professional athlete, and recruiting was carried on in all the many corners of the vast and complex country); the name was sufficient to focus the passion, and that is all any true fan needs. As those devoted to baseball know, not all members of the House of David baseball team were Jewish (in fact, none of them were; the "Yiddische Curver," the immortal Barney Pilty, belonged to some other outfit entirely). And down through the years people named Brobdignagian and Leviathanowitz have battled in the trenches for the greater glory of the Fighting Irish. Devotion to sports is usually more intense than religious tradition, affiliation, or even principle. Reggie White, the diplomat and defensive end for the Green Bay Packers, a Christian man like General Charles Gordon but much, much larger, recently said something like, "I am a Christian role model, and every time I get the chance I hit them as hard as I can." Now that he mentions it, it is true that Christianity has a long and complex pedigree of violence, which seems odd in light of the fact that when it started out Christianity was very much on the short end of the stick. But it is unfortunately true that people do not always learn not to do unto others by being done unto, and some idealists choose to try to bring the kingdom of God about more quickly by setting off bombs in department stores. I do not mean to single out Christianity in this regard, for until recently all the major religions except Buddhism were open to such criticism. Some Buddhists too now see the wisdom in fighting either for or against hegemony, and in places like Cambodia they have made up for lost time. But we were talking about sports, and how religion got into it I'm sure I don't know.

Many people feel that sailing (it used to be called yachting, but that conjures images of Commodore Vanderbilt in immaculate white ducks and blue blazer lounging on the fantail of his J-boat) is not an athletic endeavor, and indeed there is little that is more relaxing than drifting along on Moonlight Bay. But there are times when exertion, concentration, and above all, guts are needed, all excellent competitive qualities.

Once I was in the airport in Rome, on my way to India and waiting for my next flight, when I glanced at a newspaper and found an item there about a Bengali man who had undertaken the perilous journey from Calcutta to Colombo in a small sailboat. The point of the article was that the boat had been driven ashore in a storm, the three crew members rescued, but their adventure abruptly ended. It was my old friend Jyoti, as high-spirited a citizen as one could wish, who was the sailor. Although Jyoti loved the water, he had little experience of it. He bought a boat anyway, moved by the challenge that most Bengalis seem to find in life, persuaded two daring but equally inexperienced friends to come along, and off they went. I saw this little boat later, or what was left of her, moored beside the restaurant that Jyoti had opened on a hulk of a huge dhow that was anchored in the Hughli River in Calcutta. It was a most exotic setting, and the food excellent, if you went at night and could not see the indescribable things floating past on the current. Maybe Jyoti and his friends did not realize that Manu had his reasons, when he said that seafarers—together with people who argue with their fathers, those who make bows and arrows, and those who have swollen glands— are excluded from certain Vedic rituals. Or maybe he didn't care.

Vive la Difference

◇◇◇

*In which the author relaxes, puts his feet up,
and reflects on his wanderings.*

It is possible to say that the thing I missed most in India, along with the advent of the Beatles, was the feeling of the holidays. It is not that American holidays are missing from the Indian calendar, which seeks to recognize any and all holidays, thus resulting in four working days a month for all those who are observant of Hinduism, Islam, Christanity, Judaism, Buddhism, and patriotism. In fact, those who associate with Americans a lot have begun to celebrate "Santa Claus Puja," for the good reason that Indians, objective observers and experienced in this matter of holidays, see what is to be seen: a fat, jolly, generous gentleman, somewhat on the order of Ganesha, the elephant-headed son of Shiva, who overcomes obstacles and is liberal with the merchandise also, whom it hurts no one to recognize once a year. This realism has been increasing in the United States also, and has taken its purest form in the case of Thanksgiving, which, as its name implies, once was meant to acknowledge the generosity of God, but which has come, in these latter days, to be merely a time for ritually stuffing oneself to the point of immobility. Thanksgiving itself used to be known as The Start of the Holiday Season, as you may remember, but some years ago that was moved back to Halloween.

Halloween, in its turn, used to be the time when you went home from school or playing field after dark in a warm sweater on an achingly autumnal evening with the dry, sweet smell of woodsmoke and fallen leaves in the air. Before that it was the Vigil of All Saints' Day, as assigned by Gregory III in the eighth century, and before that it was a time when witches and goblins and other agents of the supernatural would come around to destroy your crops and steal your infants and generally raise hell with the environment; time, it is easy to see, in its cyclical fashion, has put the festival back into these types of adult hands again. Furthermore, in New York, where it is difficult to keep such things straight, Halloween and Thanksgiving at some point in time got confused with each other, and according to an article on the subject in the *Encyclopedia Britannica*, "[Thanksgiving] was celebrated by companies of fantastically costumed people who paraded noisily through the streets," though it is of course possible that the *Britannica* had just come in from Chicago on your average Thursday afternoon.

Actually, New York cannot be blamed entirely for the confusion, for Thanksgiving has always been a slippery kind of day. Neither Lincoln nor Roosevelt could get it to sit still on the calendar, and it was not until 1941 that Congress, superior in numbers, surrounded it and nailed it once and for all to the fourth Thursday of November. But while they were occupied with this one, all the others began to slip. Some, like Patriots' Day (which has almost nothing to do with the football team), were lost altogether, while others — Columbus Day, for example — drifted around until they ran aground against a weekend; and some — Washington's and Lincoln's Birthdays come to mind — fused together in a way I have never understood and sank to the bottom.

So while in India there is no Thankgiving in the form in which we know it (there being a dearth of turkeys), and no Halloween to begin it (though there are goblins and fantastically costumed people in plenty), there is in Calcutta a holiday season, with similarities to and differences from our own.

The closest thing to Christmas, religious overtones apart, is the autumn festival of the goddess Durga, the *Durga Puja*. It is at a time when the weather has cooled off, everybody feels good, and there is cause and means for celebration. The goddess, who is the beloved daugh-

ter of "Everybody's House," has come for a visit home
from the place where her husband Shiva sits, austerely
meditating and not paying any attention to her at all, in
the high mountains. It has been a whole year since they
saw her last, and everybody exchanges gaily wrapped
gifts and has big dinners, and the kids come with their
kids to visit, and, like Christmas, it is warm and wonderful and a huge relief when it is over. The Calcutta
bazaars, the permanent markets (there are also daily and
weekly markets for perishables and other things), are full
of goods and of shoppers, and if you look into the open
doors of the cloth shops in particular, you will see a row
of women seated on benches, others standing behind
them, as in front of them kneeling clerks are throwing
bolts of cloth across the canvas floor. A scarlet Benarasi
sari might cross a gold silk from Mysore, and a silver-
threaded one may lie athwart another of royal blue; the
women themselves are dressed in rich silks and bro-
cades, and the effect is festive and stunning. It is a wonderful time of year. Strangers smile and exchange
greetings on the street.

Puja shopping also, like holiday shopping in this country, has its hazards. An ancient newspaper clipping entitled "Roving Report on the Puja Bazaar" surfaced
recently. Although journalistic English in India has im-
proved in the intervening years, in nuance if not in color,

the situation described is the same. The brief report reads, in part:

> The crowds are so dense that . . . it is difficult to walk, even on pavements. Some are separated from the rest of their members and lost, some lose purse by skilful tact of pickpockets. . . . Some buy things on misapprehension which are not original. . . . The stores are full of . . . women with their male members.

Things are the same in India, and they are different, too.

EPILOGUE

◇◇◇

My dog, Nikki, and I don't go much of anywhere these days, in our *vana-prastha,* our retirement. We used to like to sail (well, Nikki always preferred my cousin's cruiser, the Etta G., with its spacious cockpit), but now we find it preferable to sit on the deck of our house and watch Loraine puttering in the garden, and look at the little catboat we built some years ago tugging gently at her mooring, waiting for my grandchildren to put some sail on her. (Nikki's part in the boat's building consisted largely of telling me she was sick and tired of listening to power tools, and it was time to throw her a stick.) Once in a while Nikki will get up with a groan and stroll out in her arthritic way to meet some visitor, just as I do, giving a wag or two of her tail if it turns out to be a really favorite person. Manu enjoins us hermits to be hospitable (we should "honor the people who come to visit us"), and it is amazing how many chances you get to do that, if you live on Cape Cod.

I do still go to India once in a while. But my house, with its Cape Cod lawn (i.e., crabgrass and sand) and its small echoes of my childhood, gets harder to leave all the time. And it is not true that the world is shrinking. If it were, then why would India get farther and farther away? The trip that forty years ago was overnight on an easygoing freighter now takes a cramped airplane several weeks if the weather is good.

Besides, what I nostalgically think of as my mind can make the trip instantly, and does, with or without cause. The India that it finds is sometimes more comfortable than the one at the other end of the airplane ride. It is certainly not the one that you can read about in American newspapers, which is touchy, materialistic, and not a little vain; if one were to add proud, individualistic, patriotic, and preachy, it would sound very much like we were describing ourselves, which we might very well be. We as a nation have been unreasonably annoyed by India since the days of Krishna Menon, India's first U.N. ambassador, who would insist on the moral high ground and thereby drive everybody else, who thought they were there first, to distraction. This does not mean, of course, that we think alike; even twins, to say nothing of more distant siblings, are individuals.

In any case, Manu tells me that the way I should be hospitable to those who come to my hermitage is with the vegetables and fruits that grow above the ground, and indeed I try to do that (though these guests usually expect lobster). Indeed, among the nice things about old age is the fact that there is time to scratch around in the dirt, growing the things that provide this hospitality; things that grow beneath the ground are in my sandy soil almost impossible, anyway. There are numerous other nice things, too: Nikki and I can hear or not hear, as we choose; we can go to bed when we want to, or let our hair grow long, or be forgetful or crotchety. As Manu puts it, hermits "may roll about on the ground all day or stand on tiptoe."

We can take that trip to India (Nikki, I suspect, would rather lope through her ancestral forests), or anywhere else that we have known in space or time or memory, instantly, staring into the middle distance and choosing whether to respond to stimuli. And it is my constant amazement and delight that in that place nothing ever changes, and the smiles of friends and other enchanted things are as warm as ever they were.

BIBLIOGRAPHIC NOTE

IT IS THE NATURE of books that often those read many years ago will have left indelible impressions, even though their authors and titles may be just beyond the reach of where you are standing. Others, such as Harold Isaacs' *Scratches on Our Minds* (New York: John Day, 1959) and J. R. Ackerley's *Hindoo Holiday* (New York: Poseidon Press, 1952), may provide you with points of departure for your own flights of fancy. And still others will have contributed very directly and materially to your book.

First on such a list might be Wendy Doniger's excellent translation of the Sanskrit *The Laws of Manu* (with Brian K. Smith. London: Penguin, 1991. ©1991 by Wendy Doniger and Brian K. Smith. Reprinted by permission of the authors.); the author's debt to Professor Doniger and to her books is obvious. A book indispensable for serious and also nonserious students of India is *Hobson-Jobson* (which title the book itself defines as "A native festal excitement"), *A Glossary of Anglo-Indian Words and Phrases, and of Kindred Terms, Etymological, Historical, Geographical, and Discursive,* by Colonel Henry Yule and A. C. Burnell (the edition I have used is edited by William Crooke and published by Munshiram Manoharlal of New Delhi, 1968); it is in fact a compendium of lore and anecdote, and a browser's delight. And while it would be possible to mention all the many books of social regulation that go under the general heading of *dharmashastra,* a great scholar by the name of P. V. Kane has done it all for us, and collected the gleaning in seven fat volumes entitled *History of Dharmashastra* (Pune: Bhandarkar Oriental Research Institute, 1941–62). It might be a surprise to some that Herodotus appears from time to time. This is both because of the observations on India that appear in *The History,* and because of the excellent recent translation of that text by David Grene (Chicago: University of Chicago Press, 1987).

There are throughout the current book some references and asides that might warrant further checking, either from curiosity or disbelief. Such a book might be John H. Waller, *Gordon of Khartoum: The Saga of a Victorian Hero* (New York: Atheneum, 1988). There are some very special books, for whose existence the reader will probably have to take my word, which have one way or another found their way into these pages. These are such as Constance E. Gordon's *Khana Kitab: Anglo-Indian Cuisine and Domestic Economy* (Calcutta and Simla: Thacker, Spink, and Co., 1913), Grace Thompson Seton's *Yes, Lady Sahib: A Woman's Adventures with Mysterious India* (London: Hodder and Stoughton, 1925), and Niccolao Manucci, *Storia do Mogor* (translated by William Irvine; Calcutta: Editions Indian, reprint 1965, 3 vols.).

There are many books and articles to which I have made passing reference. These include Henry David Thoreau's *Walden,* the section called "The Pond in Winter" in particular, and his *Cape Cod* also; A. K. Ramanujan's wonderful collection *Folktales from India* (New York: Pantheon, 1991), especially "The Serpent Mother"; Zareer Masani's *Indian Tales from the Raj* (Berkeley: University of California Press, 1987); Alexander Frater's charming *Chasing the Monsoon* (New York: Knopf, 1991); Chet Raymo's column "Science Musings," that appears regularly in *The Boston Globe;* James Gleick's *Chaos* (New York: Penguin, 1988); and Elizabeth B. Moynihan's lovely book *Paradise as a Garden* in Persian and Mughal India (New York: George Brazilier, 1979). Eric Solomon's "Jews, Baseball, and the American Novel" in *Arete,* Vol. I, no. 2 (1984), and Moti Nandy's "Football and Nationalism," in Geeti Sen, ed., *The Calcutta Psyche* (Delhi: India International Center, 1990/91) have contributed; Robert Hendrickson's *Salty Words* was published in New York by Hearst Marine Books in 1984. And finally, here and there, it goes without saying, lie references fanciful and otherwise to William Dwight Whitney's *Sanskrit Grammar* (Cambridge: Harvard University Press, 1925): it could not be otherwise.

ACKNOWLEDGMENTS

I SHOULD LIKE TO recognize a number of people, a rather large number for such a small book, who have contributed in substantial ways to it. It would please Manu that they can be divided up into three categories.

The first is made up of those old friends who have over many years provided encouragement, advice (sometimes, always to my regret, not followed), balance, and questions. In it are those to whom the book is dedicated; in it also are that great classicist David Grene, my deeply mourned friend the poet and scholar A. K. Ramanujan, who read parts of the book and gave occasional little puffs of laughter, the Indianist Wendy Doniger, to whom my personal and scholarly debts are very great, as has been seen, and who has followed this book along its tortuous path since its inception, my friend and neighbor the writer Larry Ramin, and my old friends and former colleagues Clint Seely and Gwen Layne.

The second category is of those friends made over the years in India, who have provided me with many of the insights, asides, remonstrations, and general instruction that find their way into the book, sometimes attributed and sometimes not. My old friends Leonard A. Gordon and Somdev Bhattacharya have given me much welcome advice and support over the years. These would include Naresh and Chinu Guha, and Pabitra and Maithili Sarkar of Calcutta, Pradeep Mehendiratta and his family, of New Delhi, and Jyoti and Meenakshi Datta, currently of New York. They also include the late Gordon Fairbanks, who in fact appears in the book from time to time, and Dr. Herbert Benson, although I've known him only in this country; I am indebted to Herb, who has written several books on the "Relaxation Response" and directs a program in hypertension at Harvard and at Beth Israel/NE Deaconess Hospital, particularly for the Pan Am story. The friend who is referred to as the Rajkumar, in the House of Mayurbhanj, is the late Svarup Bhanjdeo, a prince of a man in more ways than one.

And then there are the many people, ranging from old friends to professional editors, and some in whom are combined both of these, who had directly to do with the book. I would begin with my witty, compassionate, and thoroughly effective agent, Virginia Kidd, and Robert A.

Rubin, Memsy Price, and Antonia Fusco of Algonquin Books: all of them worked long and hard on the book, but it has been Antonia who has done the grinding work of editing, bringing an amorphous mass of material to as fine a point as possible; I have learned a great deal from her simultaneous rigor and courtesy. There have been many others as well, including Penny Kaiserlian of the University of Chicago Press, who read some of the essays early on and took an interest in them, and Diane Mines, who helped prepare one phase of the manuscript.

Obviously hardly least is the wife who wends her seemingly unappreciated way through the pages of the book. Loraine has seen us through some rough times, and some good ones, too. It is fine that she too has found a few chuckles here.

There are many people who have provided me with critical support during illness, ups during downs, and laughs when there seemed little to laugh about (they were always right). I have not mentioned them because I could not, for want of space, and cannot, for want of words. I have tried to sort this out by limiting names to those who have specifically helped with the book. The others will have to be satisfied to have their names written on my heart.

Centerville, Massachusetts